TABE 9 & 10 Applied Math
Practice Test Book
Study Guide with 400 TABE Math
Questions for Levels E, M, D, and A

The TABE Test is a trademark of Data Recognition Corporation, which is not affiliated with or endorses this publication.

TABE 9 & 10 Applied Math Practice Test Book: Study Guide with 400 TABE Math Questions for Levels E, M, D, and A

© COPYRIGHT 2018

Exam SAM Study Aids & Media dba www.examsam.com

All rights reserved. No part of this publication may be reproduced, stored in a retrieval system, or transmitted, in any form or by any means, electronic, mechanical, photocopying, recording, or otherwise, without the prior written permission of the copyright owner.

ISBN-13: 978-1-949282-00-9

ISBN-10: 1-949282-00-7

For information on bulk discounts, please contact us at: email@examsam.com

The TABE Test is a trademark of Data Recognition Corporation, which is not affiliated with or endorses this publication.

How to Use This Publication

The first 150 problems in this book are organized into four sections: (1) Number Operations, Estimation, Computation in Context, and Problem Solving; (2) Measurement, Geometry & Spatial Sense; (3) Data Analysis, Statistics & Probability; and (4) Algebra, Functions & Patterns.

You should work through the concepts in practice questions 1 to 150 first. Pay special attention to the tips and hints after each question in these four sections. The comments after each question tell you how to solve each type of problem that you will see on the real test and give you strategies for the day of your exam.

The five practice tests at the end of the publication are like the actual exam, so they have questions from all four levels of difficulty. You should attempt the practice tests after you have studied all of the other material in the book. To simulate the real exam, you should allow 50 minutes to take each of the practice tests.

The book includes problems for all of the levels of the TABE 9 & 10 tests: Easy (E) Medium (M), Difficult (D), and Advanced (A). The level of each question is indicated by the letters E, M, D, or A after the text of each problem.

On the real exam, you will be allowed to use a calculator and scratch paper to solve the problems. On the real test, you will not be penalized for guessing, so you should try to answer every question.

The answers and solutions for all of the practice test questions are provided at the end of the last practice exam.

Please note that for geometry questions, you should use 3.14 for π. Also note that the drawings in this publication are not to scale.

Formulas are provided after questions 1 to 150 as all of the concepts are introduced in these questions.

Should you wish to refer to the formulas later, please see the appendix to the book.

Free Basic Math Review

This study guide assumes some knowledge of basic math skills, such as addition, subtraction, multiplication, division, percentages, and decimals.

If you have difficulties with basic math problems or if you have been out of school for a while, you may wish to review our free basic math problems before taking the practice tests in this book.

The free review problems can be found at: www.examsam.com/math/numerical-skills/

TABLE OF CONTENTS

How to Use This Publication — i

Number Operations, Estimation, Computation in Context, and Problem Solving

Operations with Whole Numbers — 1

Fractions, Decimals, and Percentages — 2

Units of Money — 3

Units of Time — 3

Problems with Two or More Operations — 3

Negative Numbers – Multiplication — 4

Averages — 4

Ratios, Proportions, and Rates — 4

Adding and Subtracting Fractions with Common Denominators — 5

Adding Commonly-Known Decimals — 5

Adding Commonly-Known Percentages — 6

Multiplying Mixed Numbers by Whole Numbers — 6

Fractions with Unlike Denominators — 6

Finding the Best Price — 6

Calculating Discounts — 6

Calculating Markups — 7

Reverse Percentages — 7

Productions Rates by Time and Units — 7

Measurement, Geometry & Spatial Sense

Converting Distances — 8

Mixed Unit Calculations — 8

Conversions within Systems of Measurement — 8

Fractions as Units of Measurement — 8

Liquid Measurements — 9

Midpoint and Distance Formulas — 9

Slope and Slope-Intercept	9
Equations of Lines	10
Triangle – Area	10
Hypotenuse Length	11
Triangle Laws	11
Degrees in a Circle	11
Circles – Area	11
Circles – Circumference	11
Rectangles – Area	11
Rectangles – Perimeter	12
Volume of Rectangular Shapes	12
Volume of Cubes	12
Volume of Spheres	12
Volume of Cylinders	13
Volume of Cones	13
Using Formulas in Reverse	13
Converting Measurements and Volumes	13
Liquid Measurements with Mixed Units	14
Finding Errors in Calculations	14
Calculating Differences in Volumes	15

Data Analysis, Statistics & Probability

Mean	15
Mode	15
Median	16
Range	16
Calculating Mean with a Missing Value	16
Mean and Median – Advanced Questions	16
Probability	17

Working with Charts, Graphs, and Tables	18

Algebra, Functions, and Patterns

Expressions with One Variable	20
Expressions with Two Variables	20
Roots and Radicals	21
Exponent Laws	22
Simplifying Rational Algebraic Expressions	23
Factoring Polynomials	24
Equivalent Expressions	24
Expanding Polynomials	24
Linear Equations	25
Algebraic Functions	26
Logarithmic Functions	28
Quadratic Equations	28
Linear Inequalities	29
Quadratic Inequalities	29
Systems of Equations	30
Patterns, Series, and Sequences	30

TABE 9 & 10 Practice Tests 1 to 5

TABE 9 & 10 Practice Test 1	31
TABE 9 & 10 Practice Test 2	39
TABE 9 & 10 Practice Test 3	47
TABE 9 & 10 Practice Test 4	56
TABE 9 & 10 Practice Test 5	64

Answers, Solutions, and Explanations

Answers and Solutions to Questions 1 to 150	72
Practice Test 1 – Solutions and Explanations	91
Practice Test 2 – Solutions and Explanations	97

Practice Test 3 – Solutions and Explanations	102
Practice Test 4 – Solutions and Explanations	108
Practice Test 5 – Solutions and Explanations	113
Answer Key – All Questions	118
Appendix – Applied Mathematics Formula Sheet	126

Number Operations, Estimation, Computation in Context, and Problem Solving

1) A company sells electronics online. The annual sales for the first three years of business were: $25,135, $32,787, and $47,004. What were the total sales for the past three years? **(E)**
   A) $101,326 B) $104,916 C) $104,926 D) $104,944

This is a question on adding whole numbers. The problem is asking for the total for all three years, so add the three figures together.

2) A customer gives the cashier $50 to pay for the items he purchased, which total $41.28. How much change should be given to the customer? **(E)**
   A) $7.82 B) $8.18 C) $8.27 D) $8.72

This is a question on subtracting whole numbers. To calculate the change, you need to take the amount of money the customer gives the cashier and subtract the amount of the purchase.

3) A car salesperson earns a $175 referral fee on every customer who accepts a customer service upgrade. The salesperson referred 8 customers for the service upgrade this month. How much did the salesperson earn in referral fees for the month? **(E)**
   A) $1050 B) $1200 C) $1225 D) $1400

This is a question on multiplying whole numbers. Multiplication problems will often include the words 'each' or 'every.' Multiply the amount of the referral fee by the number of customers to solve.

4) An employee's weekly pay is $535.50 and she works 30 hours per week. How much is she paid per hour? **(E)**
   A) $17.83 B) $17.84 C) $17.85 D) $18.34

This is a question on dividing whole numbers. Division problems will often include the word 'per.' Divide the total weekly amount by the number of hours to solve.

5) Business losses are represented as negative numbers, while business profits are represented as positive numbers. A business makes the following profits and losses during a four week period: −$286, $953, $1502, and −$107. What was the total business profit or loss during these four weeks? **(E)**
   A) $2,026 B) $2,062 C) $2,080 D) −$2,026

This is a question on adding negative numbers. When you have to add a negative number to a positive number, you are subtracting. So, add the business profits and subtract the business losses to solve.

6) Location below sea level is represented as a negative number. The location below sea level of Lake Alto is −35 meters. The location below sea level of Lake Bajo is 62 meters deeper than Lake Alto. What figure represents the location below sea level for Lake Bajo? **(E)**
   A) −97 B) 97 C) −62 D) −27

This is a question on subtracting negative numbers. The facts state that the location below sea level of Lake Bajo is 62 meters deeper than Lake Alto, so we need to subtract this figure from the location below sea level of Lake Alto. The location below sea level of Lake Alto is a negative number, so you are subtracting a negative from a negative.

7) A company has completed 3/5 of a project. What figure below expresses the project completion amount as a decimal number? **(E)**
   A) 0.06
   B) 0.60
   C) 1.67
   D) 3.00

> This is a question on changing fractions to decimals. To express a fraction as a decimal, treat the line in the fraction as the division symbol and divide accordingly. Remember to be careful with the decimal placement in your final answer.

8) A teacher reports attendance as a decimal figure, calculated as the number of students attending divided into the total number of students in the class. This week, the attendance was 0.55. What percentage best represents the attendance for this week? **(E)**
   A) 0.55%
   B) 5.50%
   C) 55.0%
   D) 55.5%

> This is a question on changing decimals to percentages. To express a decimal number as a percentage, move the decimal point two places to the right. Then add the percent sign.

9) An employee has used up 5/14 of his vacation days. Approximately what percentage of vacation days has the employee already used? **(M)**
   A) 0.357%
   B) 2.800%
   C) 3.571%
   D) 35.7%

> This is a question on changing fractions to decimals. Treat the line in the fraction as the division symbol and divide. Then move the decimal point two places to the right, and add the percent sign.

10) A driver has used 0.75 of the gas he last put in his car. What fraction best represents the amount of gas used? **(E)**
    A) 1/4
    B) 2/5
    C) 3/5
    D) 3/4

> This is a question on changing a decimal number to a fraction. You should be able to recognize the equivalent decimal numbers for commonly-used fractions such as ½ or ¾ for your exam. If you are unsure, perform division on the answer choices to solve.

11) It is reported that 33% of all new stores close within five years of opening. What fraction best represents this percentage? **(E)**
    A) 1/3
    B) 1/4
    C) 1/5
    D) 2/3

> This is a question on changing a percentage to a fraction. You should be able to recognize the equivalent fractions for commonly-used percentages for the test. If you are unsure of the answer, perform division on the answer choices to solve.

12) A carpet store is offering 45% off in a sale this month. What decimal number below best represents the percentage off? **(E)**
    A) 0.0045
    B) 0.0450
    C) 0.4500
    D) 4.5000

> This is a question on changing percentages to decimals. Any given percentage is out of 100%, so we divide by 100 to express a percentage as a decimal. So, move the decimal point two places to the left and remove the percent sign.

13) A bakery has to pay 36 cents for each pound of flour it buys. It decides to buy 14¼ pounds of flour today. How much will it have to pay? **(M)**
   A) $3.60   B) $5.13   C) $5.31   D) $142.50

This is a question on calculations involving units of money. Express both amounts as decimal numbers and multiply to solve.

14) A bookkeeper has just been with a client for 0.35 hours. Approximately how many minutes did the bookkeeper spend with this client? **(M)**
   A) 3.5 minutes   B) 5.8 minutes   C) 21 minutes   D) 35 minutes

This is a question on calculations involving units of time. There are 60 minutes in an hour, so multiply the minutes in the hour by the decimal number given in the problem to solve.

15) A flower store charges $24 for a small arrangement of flowers. A customer will get a $5 discount if he or she provides his or her own vase for the small arrangement. This month, there were 12 customers who ordered small arrangements and provided their own vases. How much money in total did the flower store make on arrangements sold to these 12 customers? **(M)**
   A) $228   B) $282   C) $288   D) $348

This is a question with two operations. Subtract the discount from the original price. Then multiply this figure by the number of units sold.

16) A bricklayer works for a construction company. He laid bricks for 7 hours per day for 4 days on one job. The customer was billed $45 per hour for his work, and he was paid $25 per hour. After the bricklayer's wages have been paid, how much money did the company make for his work on this job? **(M)**
   A) $175   B) $180   C) $315   D) $560

This question has three operations. First, you need to determine the total number of hours worked for the 4 days. Then calculate the profit the company makes per hour. Finally, multiply the total number of hours worked by the profit per hour to solve.

17) A pharmacist owns a local drug store. Last week, she filled 250 prescriptions in 40 hours. Assuming that each prescription takes the same amount of time, how many minutes should it take her to fill a single prescription? **(M)**
   A) 9.6 minutes   B) 6.25 minutes   C) 3.75 minutes   D) 0.16 minutes

This is a question with two operations. Since there are 60 minutes in an hour, we multiply by 60 to get the number of minutes. Then divide by the number of prescriptions to get the rate.

18) A truck driver delivered 120 orders this week. She delivered 105 of the orders on time. What percentage of the driver's orders was delivered on time? **(M)**
   A) 0.875%   B) 8.75%   C) 87.5%   D) 0.125%

This is a question with two operations. Take the amount of orders that were delivered on time and divide by the amount of total orders. Then convert to a percentage.

19) A scientist measures cell growth or attrition. Each day a measurement is taken. Cell growth is represented as a positive figure, while cell attrition is represented as a negative figure. On Monday cell growth was 27, and for all days Tuesday through Friday, cell attrition was 13 per day. What number represents total cell growth or attrition for these five days? **(E)**
A) 25   B) –25   C) 40   D) –40

This is a question on multiplying negative numbers. Cell attrition is a negative number, so perform multiplication to get the total for Tuesday through Friday. Then add the cell growth for Monday to solve.

20) A vegetable farmer works until noon each day. The chart below shows the amounts of cucumbers per hour that she picked one morning: **(M)**
7:00 to 8:00   23 cucumbers   10:00 to 11:00   24 cucumbers
8:00 to 9:00   25 cucumbers   11:00 to 12:00   22 cucumbers
9:00 to 10:00   26 cucumbers

On average, how many cucumbers did the farmer pick per hour?
A) 23   B) 24   C) 25   D) 26

This is a question on calculating averages. The average is sometimes called the arithmetic mean, so you may see both terms on the test. To find the average, you need to add all of the amounts to get the total, and then divide the total by the number of hours.

21) A local company makes one particular kind of concrete. For this concrete, 2 units of sand have to be added to every 3 units of cement powder used. A batch of this concrete that has 66 units of cement powder is being made. How many units of sand should be added to this batch? **(M)**
A) 2   B) 3   C) 22   D) 44

This is a question on a simple ratio. Take the 66 units of cement powder for the current batch and divide by the 3 units stated in the original ratio. Then multiply this result by the 2 units of sand stated in the original ratio to solve.

22) It is company policy that the ratio of employees to supervisors should be 50:1. So, for every 50 employees in a company, there should be 1 supervisor. If there are 255 employees, how many supervisors are there? **(M)**
A) 1   B) 2   C) 3   D) 5

This is another question on a simple ratio. The problem states that we are working with a ratio, so the employees and the supervisors form separate groups. First, add the two groups together. Then take the total amount of employees stated in the problem and divide this by the figure you have just calculated to get the amount of supervisors.

23) A report shows that 2 out of every 20 employees in a particular company are interested in applying for a promotion. If the company has 480 employees in total, how many employees are interested in applying for a promotion? **(M)**
A) 20   B) 24   C) 42   D) 48

This is a question on a simple proportion. Problems on proportions often use the phrase 'out of.' The problem uses the phrase '2 out of every 20 employees' so we know that there are 2 employees who form a subset within each group of 20. So, take the total number of employees and divide this by 20. Then multiply this result by the amount in the subset to solve.

24) A mechanic spent from 8:10 to 8:22 changing three wheel covers on a car. At this rate, how many wheel covers could he change per hour? **(M)**
   A) 3   B) 5   C) 15   D) 20

> This is a question on calculating a simple rate. Calculate the amount of time in minutes that was spent on the three wheel covers. Then calculate the time in minutes needed to change 1 wheel cover. Then divide this amount into 60 minutes to solve.

25) A fencing company put up $15^{2}/_{8}$ yards of fence for one customer and $13^{5}/_{8}$ yards of fence for another customer. How many yards of fence did the company put up for both customers in total? **(M)**
   A) $28^{3}/_{8}$ B) $28^{5}/_{8}$ C) $28^{7}/_{8}$ D) $28^{7}/_{16}$

> This is a question on adding fractions that have a common denominator. First, add the whole numbers that are in front of each fraction. Then add the fractions. If you have two fractions that have the same denominator, which is the number on the bottom of the fraction, you add the numerators and keep the common denominator. Then combine the new whole number and the new fraction to solve.

26) A food company fills gourmet food boxes with various products. So far today, $2^{3}/_{8}$ boxes have been filled for one order and $4^{1}/_{8}$ boxes have been filled for another order. How many total boxes have been filled so far today? **(M)**
   A) $6^{1}/_{2}$ B) $6^{1}/_{4}$ C) $6^{3}/_{4}$ D) $6^{3}/_{16}$

> This is another question on adding fractions that have a common denominator. Follow the same steps as for the previous question, but also simplify the fraction to solve. This means that you have to reduce the numerator and denominator by dividing them by the same number, which is known as a common factor.

27) A customer has just placed an order to have an awning made for his front window. According to the measurements, $5^{3}/_{16}$ yards of canvas will be needed to make the awning. However, the customer calls later to say that his initial measurement was incorrect, and only $4^{1}/_{16}$ yards of canvas is actually needed to make the awning. Which fraction below represents the amount by which the amount of canvas has been reduced? **(M)**
   A) $1^{1}/_{8}$ B) $1^{1}/_{16}$ C) $1^{1}/_{32}$ D) $1^{3}/_{16}$

> This is a question on subtracting fractions with a common denominator. First, subtract the whole numbers, and then subtract the fractions. If you have two fractions that have the same denominator, you subtract the numerators and keep the common denominator. Then simplify the fraction. Finally, combine the whole number and the simplified fraction to solve.

28) Certain additives need to be placed in a bottle to make a particular product. The company measures each additive in decimal units, with 1 unit representing the filled bottle. The bottle contains 0.25 units of additive A, 0.50 units of additive B, and 0.10 units of additive C. Which of the following represents, in terms of units, how full the bottle currently is? **(M)**
   A) 08.5   B) 0.85   C) 0.90   D) 0.95

> This is a question on adding commonly-known decimals. Add the three figures together to solve. Remember to be sure to put the decimal point in the correct place when you work out the solution.

29) A recent survey shows that 50% of your customers rated your service as excellent and 25% rated your service as very good. What percentage below represents the total amount of customers who rated your service either excellent or very good? **(M)**
   A) 25%   B) 50%   C) 75%   D) 85%

This is a question on adding commonly-known percentages. Simply add the percentages together to solve.

30) A customer has just ordered 5 units of a product. Each unit of the product takes $1\frac{1}{4}$ hours to make. How much time is needed to make this order? **(M)**
   A) 5 hours and 25 minutes
   B) 5 hours and 55 minutes
   C) 6 hours and 4 minutes
   D) 6 hours and 15 minutes

This is a question on multiplying a mixed number by a whole number of units. First, multiply the whole numbers. Then multiply the whole number of units by the fraction. Then convert this improper fraction to a mixed number. Add the whole number and the mixed number, and convert to hours and minutes to solve.

31) A dressmaker who works in a tailoring shop is trying to decide what setting to use on the sewing machine. She has tried the 1/8 inch stitch but has realized that it is too small. The stitches on the machine are sized in 1/32 increments. What size stitch should she try next? **(M)**
   A) 3/16   B) 5/32   C) 6/16   D) 6/32

This is a question on performing calculations on fractions with different denominators. Convert 1/8 to the following equivalent fraction: 1/8 = ?/32

32) Amal runs a souvenir store that sells key rings. She can get 50 key rings from her first supplier for 50 cents each. She can get the same 50 keys rings from her second supplier for $30 in total or from her third supplier for $27.50. How much will she pay if she gets the best deal? **(M)**
   A) $25.00   B) $25.25   C) $25.50   D) $27.50

This is a question on finding the best deal when you have to perform a one-step calculation. Read the facts carefully, work out the total prices for all three suppliers, and then compare prices.

33) A budget hotel charges $45 per night or $280 per week. If a guest stays at the hotel for 9 nights, what is the least that he will pay for his stay? **(M)**
   A) $280   B) $315   C) $325   D) $370

This is a question on finding the best deal when you have to perform two-step calculations. Determine the duration of the stay in weeks and nights. Then add the cost for 1 week to the cost for 2 days to solve.

34) The price of an item is normally $15, but customers with a loyalty card can purchase it at the discounted price of $12. What percentage best represents the discount awarded to these customers? **(M)**
   A) 3%   B) 5%   C) 15%   D) 20%

This is a question on calculating the percentage of a discount. Divide the dollar amount of the discount by the original price to get the percentage of the discount.

35) A retail ceramics store sells mugs and bowls. It buys one type of mug for $3 and sells it for $9. It uses the same percentage mark up on one type of bowl that it buys for $4. What figure below represents the sales price of the bowl? **(M)**
A) $6 B) $8 C) $12 D) $16

This is a question on calculating a markup. You need to calculate the percentage for the markup on the first product and apply this percentage markup to the second product. Remember to use the percentage markup, rather than a dollar value. You may need the following formulas if you don't already know how to calculate markup: Dollar value of markup = Sales price in dollars − Cost in dollars; Percentage markup = Dollar value of markup ÷ Cost in dollars

36) A company got $20 off of an order. This amounted to a 25% discount off the order. What would the company have paid without the discount? **(M)**
A) $4 B) $5 C) $25 D) $80

This is a question on calculating a reverse percentage. To calculate a reverse percentage you need to divide, rather than multiply. So, take the dollar value of the discount and divide by the percentage to solve.

37) A company that fabricates cleaning products begins to make the first batch of products on Monday at 10:30 am. The actual production time is 3 hours and 25 minutes. This is followed by a bottling and labeling process that takes 1 hour and 40 minutes and a packaging process that takes a further 26 hours. If production keeps to this schedule, when will the first batch be ready for shipment? **(D)**
A) Tuesday at 12:30 pm
B) Tuesday at 3:55 pm
C) Tuesday at 5:35 pm
D) Wednesday at 3:55 pm

This is a question on calculating the hours and minutes that have passed since the start of a job or process. Calculate the total time for the entire process and add to the starting time to solve.

38) Maria sells soft drinks in a convenience store that she runs. She can buy 240 soft drinks from one supplier for 25 cents each or from a different supplier for $58 for all 240 drinks. Both suppliers are in the same state, so she has to pay a sales tax of 6.5% on either purchase. If she chooses the best price for the soft drinks, including tax, how much will she pay in total? **(D)**
A) $58.00 B) $60.00 C) $61.77 D) $63.90

This is an advanced question on finding the best deal. Remember to add the dollar amount of the sales tax to both calculations for this problem.

39) A picture framing store can make 20 small frames in 4 days or 21 large frames in 3 days. A customer has just placed an order with for 40 small frames and 64 large ones. Approximately how many days will it take to make them all? **(D)**
A) 7 B) 11 C) 14 D) 17

This is a question on calculating production rates by unit. Determine the unit rates per day for each of the products by dividing the output by the number of days. Then divide the rates into the amount of items ordered to solve.

40) The report on a production order shows that 12.5% of the work has been completed in the past 4 days. If work continues at the same rate, how many more days will be required in order to finish the order? **(D)**
A) 3   B) 4   C) 28   D) 32

> This is a question on calculating rate by time. Calculate the percentage of work completed per day, and then determine how many days are needed for the job.

Measurement, Geometry & Spatial Sense

41) A land surveyor must measure the distance between landmarks. She has measured a distance between two landmarks and discovered that it is 538 feet. What is the approximate distance between the landmarks in terms of meters? **(D)**
A) 45   B) 164   C) 1367   D) 1765

> This is a question on using a formula with a measurement. Use the following formula and multiply to solve: 1 foot = 0.3048 meters

42) A physical therapist measures how far her clients are able to walk during each session. One client walked 123 feet and 6 inches during his first session and 138 feet and 8 inches during his second session. What is the combined total of the distance walked for the two sessions? **(M)**
A) 261 feet 24 inches
B) 261 feet 6 inches
C) 262 feet 8 inches
D) 262 feet 2 inches

> This is a question on performing a calculation with mixed units. It is usually easiest to perform one calculation with the feet and another with the inches. You may need to convert the total inches back to feet and inches if there are more than 12 inches in the second calculation.

43) A nutritionist advises clients and sells supplements to them. A box containing the supplements weighs 8 pounds and 5 ounces when full. The box itself weighs 7 ounces when it is empty. Each supplement weighs 0.75 ounces. About how many supplements should be in the box? **(D)**
A) 168   B) 177   C) 178   D) 186

> This is a question on performing conversions within systems of measurement. Here we have to convert between pounds and ounces. Convert the total weight of the product (excluding the box weight) to ounces then divide the total ounces by the ounces per unit to solve. 1 pound = 16 ounces

44) A garden store fertilizes and treats customers' lawns. One customer wants to fertilize and treat his lawn, which is $50\frac{1}{4}$ feet by $60\frac{1}{4}$ feet in size. The cost of the fertilizer and treatment is $5.25 per square yard. To the nearest dollar, how much will it cost the customer to fertilize and treat his lawn? **(D)**
A) $177   B) $1,766   C) $5,298   D) $15,895

> This is a question on working with quantities that contain fractions. Convert the mixed numbers to decimals and multiply. Then convert to square yards and solve. 1 square yard = 9 square feet

45) It is company policy to have at least 60 yards of dark black yarn in stock at the start of every month. Inventory has been taken this morning and there are 2 balls of dark black yarn that are 75 inches each and 4 balls of dark black yarn that are 25¼ inches each in stock. This yarn must be purchased in 5-yard-long balls. How many balls of yarn should be purchased in order to replenish the stock? **(D)**
A) 10   B) 11   C) 33   D) 36

This is a question on working with fractional units. Calculate the amount of remaining stock in inches, and then convert from inches to yards. Then calculate the amount required to restock. Remember that it is not possible to buy a fractional part of a ball, so you have to round up to solve.

46) A company that manufactures liquid cosmetics needs to test a 0.75 gram sample of an active ingredient of a liquid cosmetic. The correct concentration ratio is 50 milligrams of active ingredient to 1.5 milliliters of liquid. How many milliliters of liquid should be added to the sample? **(D)**
A) 0.000015   B) 0.000225   C) 15.0   D) 22.5

This is a question on converting grams to milligrams. Convert to grams (1 gram = 1,000 milligrams). Then apply the correct ratio to solve.

47) Find the midpoint of the line segment that connects the points (5, 2) and (7, 4). **(D)**
A) (6, 3)   B) (3, 6)   C) (3.5, 5.5)   D) (12, 6)

48) If store A is represented by the coordinates (−4, 2) and store B is represented by the coordinates (8, −6), and store A and store B are connected by a line segment, what is the midpoint of this line? **(D)**

A) (2, 2)   B) (2, −2)   C) (−2, 2)   D) (−2, −2)

The midpoint of two points on a two-dimensional graph is calculated by using the midpoint formula:
$(x_1 + x_2) \div 2 , (y_1 + y_2) \div 2$

49) What is the distance between (2, 3) and (6, 7)? **(A)**
A) 4   B) 16   C) $\sqrt{16}$ D) $\sqrt{32}$

The distance formula is used to calculate the linear distance between two points on a two-dimensional graph. The two points are represented by the coordinates (x_1, y_1) and (x_2, y_2).
$d = \sqrt{(x_2 - x_1)^2 + (y_2 - y_1)^2}$

50) The measurements of a mountain can be placed on a two dimensional linear graph on which $x = 5$ and $y = 315$. If the line crosses the y axis at 15, what is the slope of this mountain? **(D)**
A) 60   B) 63   C) 300   D) 315

The slope formula: $m = \dfrac{y_2 - y_1}{x_2 - x_1}$

The slope-intercept formula: $y = mx + b$, where m is the slope and b is the y intercept.

51) Which of the following statements is true with respect to the lined graph below? **(D)**

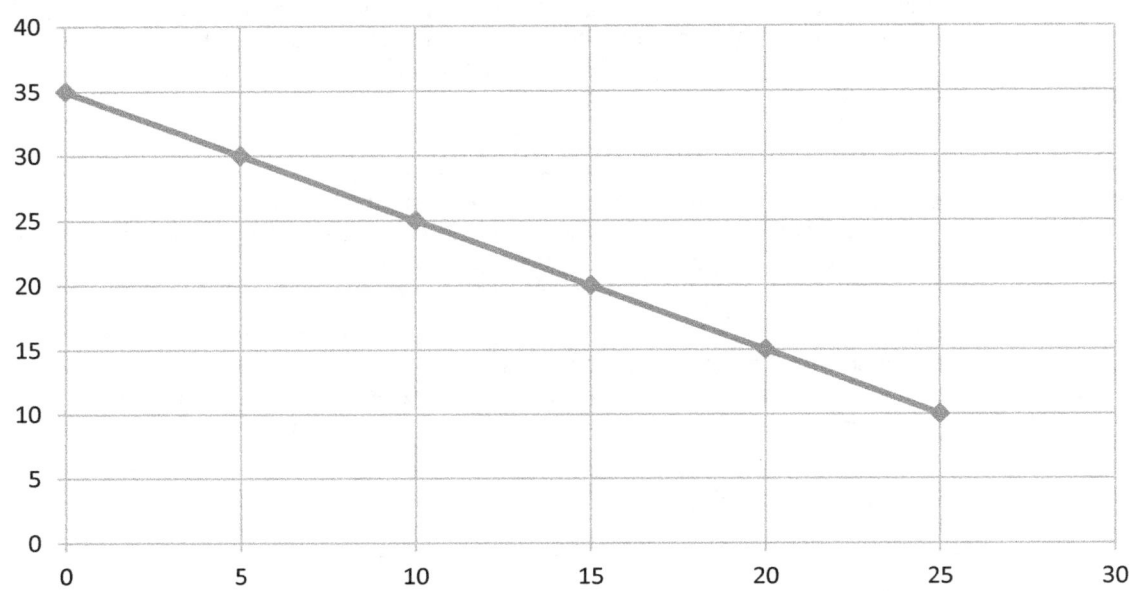

A) The line has a slope of –1 and contains point (20, 15).
B) The line has a slope of 1 and contains point (20, 15).
C) The line has a slope of –1 and contains point (15, 20).
D) The line has a slope of 1 and contains point (15, 20).

52) State the x and y intercepts that fall on the straight line represented by the equation: $y = x + 14$ **(D)**
A) (–14, 0) and (0, 14)
B) (0, 14) and (0, –14)
C) (14, 0) and (0, –14)
D) (0, –14) and (14, 0)

53) Find the x and y intercepts of the following equation: $x^2 + 2y^2 = 144$ **(A)**
A) (12, 0) and (0, $\sqrt{72}$)
B) (0, 12) and ($\sqrt{72}$, 0)
C) (0, $\sqrt{72}$) and (0, 12)
D) (12, 0) and ($\sqrt{72}$, 0)

For questions like the two above on x and y intercepts, substitute 0 for y in the equation provided to find the value of x. Then substitute 0 for x to find the value of y and solve the problem.

54) A carpenter creates triangular-shaped corner shelves from oak and other wood for sale to furniture and home stores. He needs to report the area of each shelf to the buyer as part of the sales agreement. He needs to calculate the area of a triangular-shaped shelf that has a base of 12 inches and a height of 14 inches. What is the area of this shelf in square inches? **(D)**
A) 56   B) 84   C) 168   D) 1728

Use the formula for the area of a triangle: ½ (base × height)

55) Triangle ABC is a right-angled triangle. Side A and side B form the right angle, and side C is the hypotenuse. If A = 3 and B = 2, what is the length of side C? **(A)**
   A) 5   B) $\sqrt{5}$ C) $\sqrt{13}$ D) 13

The hypotenuse is the side of the triangle that is opposite the right angle. To calculate the length of the hypotenuse in right triangles, you will need the Pythagorean Theorem. According to the theorem, the length of the hypotenuse (represented by side C) is equal to the square root of the sum of the squares of the other two sides of the triangle (represented by A and B). For any right triangle with sides A, B, and C, you need to remember this formula:
$$\text{hypotenuse length } C = \sqrt{A^2 + B^2}$$

56) A carpenter is making a special triangular-shaped corner shelf for a custom order. The customer lives in a 300-year-old house, so the walls are not completely straight and the corners are not completely square. He needs to make a triangular shelf that will have one 44° angle and one 47° angle. What is the measurement in degrees of the third angle of this shelf? **(D)**
   A) 45°   B) 45.5°   C) 89°   D) 90°

The sum of all three angles in any triangle is always equal to 180 degrees.

57) A real-estate developer has recently purchased a circular-shaped tower. The first floor of the building has been divided into 5 pie-shaped segments that join at the center of the circle. The first segment measures 82° along the outside edge. The second segment has a measurement of 79°, the third has a measurement of 46° and the fourth has a measurement of 85°. What is the measurement in degrees of outside edge the fifth segment? **(D)**
   A) 48   B) 49   C) 58   D) 68

A complete circle measures 360 degrees.

58) A building project has a circular tower. The floor of the tower, which has a 12-foot radius, needs to be filled in with concrete. In order to do this, the area of the floor of the tower needs to be calculated. What is the approximate area of the floor of the tower in square feet? **(A)**
   A) 452.16   B) 376.80   C) 226.08   D) 37.68

This is a question on calculating the area of a circle. The formula for the area of a circle is as follows: circle area ≈ 3.14 × (radius)^2

59) A technician measures the wear on tractor tires. In order to determine the rate of wear, the circumference of each tire must be determined first. The tire currently being measured has a diameter of 46.5 inches. What is the circumference? **(A)**
   A) 23.500 inches   B) 73.005 inches   C) 146.01 inches   D) 292.02 inches

This is a question on calculating the circumference of a circle. Circumference ≈ 3.14 × diameter

60) Becky is making a patchwork quilt that is going to be 6 feet long and 5 feet wide. What will the surface area of the quilt be in square feet? **(D)**
   A) 11   B) 22   C) 25   D) 30

This is a question on calculating the area of a rectangle. Area of a rectangle = length × width

61) A fence needs to be put around a field that is 12 yards long and 9 yards wide. What figure below best represents the perimeter of this field in yards? **(D)**
   A) 21   B) 42   C) 54   D) 72

This is a question on calculating the perimeter of a rectangle. Remember not to confuse area and perimeter as they are different calculations. Perimeter of a rectangle = 2 × (length + width)

62) A circular fish pond is being designing for your local park. The pond has an area of about 78.5 square feet. What is the approximate diameter of the pond? **(D)**
   A) 5 feet   B) 10 feet   C) 15.7 feet   D) 25 feet

You need to use the formula in reverse for this question, so use 3.14 for π and divide by 3.14, instead of multiplying by 3.14. Remember that diameter is double the radius, so if the radius is 3 feet, for example, the diameter is 6 feet. Remember that the formula is: circle area ≈ 3.14 × (radius)^2.

63) A rectangular vegetable garden has an area of 360 square feet. If the length of the garden is 30 feet, what is the width of the garden? **(A)**
   A) 12 feet   B) 24 feet   C) 115 feet   D) 150 feet

This is another question on rearranging a formula. The area of a rectangle = length × width. Here, we are given the area, so we need to divide that by the length to solve.

64) A tank that holds dye is 5 feet wide, 8 feet long, and 3 feet high. How many cubic feet of dye can the tank hold when it is completely full? **(A)**
   A) 15   B) 24   C) 40   D) 120

The length, width, and height are different measurements, so we need the formula for the volume of a rectangular solid or box: volume = *length × width × height*

65) A cube footrest has a side length of 18 inches. How many cubic inches of filling should be placed inside the footrest? **(A)**
   A) 5,832   B) 729   C) 324   D) 72

For this problem, we need to calculate the volume of a cube. The formula for the volume of a cube is as follows: cube volume = (*length of side*)^3

66) A company processes dairy products. Milk is stored in a spherical storage tank that is 72 inches across on the inside. The tank is now 80% full of milk. What is the volume of the milk in the tank? **(A)**
   A) 156,267   B) 156,627   C) 159,333   D) 195,333

This is a question on calculating volume. You need the following formula: Volume of a sphere ≈ 4/3 × 3.14 × radius^3. Use the formula and multiply by the percentage stated in the problem.

67) A cylindrical tank has a 5 meter radius and is 21 meters in height. What is the volume of the tank? **(A)**
A) 329.70   B) 1648.5   C) 549.50   D) 659.40

This is another question on calculating volume. Cylinder volume ≈ 3.14 × radius² × height. Substitute the values into the formula, and perform the operations in the formula to solve.

68) A confection company manufactures three different sizes of ice cream cones. The large cones are 6 inches high and have a 1.5 inch radius, the medium cones are 5 inches high and have a 1 inch radius, and the small cones are 4 inches high and have a 0.5 inch radius. What is the difference between the volume in cubic inches of the large cone and the medium cone? **(A)**
A) 4.19   B) 5.23   C) 8.90   D) 14.13

This is a question on calculating differences in volumes. Cone volume ≈ (3.14 × radius² × height) ÷ 3. Calculate the difference between the volumes of the two cones to solve.

69) A building contractor is laying wooden parquet pieces on a floor. The wooden part of the floor will cover an area that measures 8 feet long by 4 feet wide. Each wooden parquet piece measures 12 inches by 6 inches. What is the minimum number of wooden parquet pieces that will be needed in order to cover the wooden part of the floor? **(A)**
A) 16   B) 32   C) 48   D) 64

Determine how many wooden pieces will fit along the length of the floor. Next, determine how many wooden pieces can fit along the width. Finally, multiply to solve.

70) A painter is painting a wall that is 16 feet long and 11 feet high. She needs to calculate the surface area of the wall in order to know how much paint to buy. What is the surface area of the wall in square feet? **(D)**
A) 54   B) 121   C) 176   D) 256

Don't let the fact that this is a wall confuse you. You still need to calculate the area. Which previous formula should you use?

71) A rectangular solid container needs to be filled with a liquid substance. The length of the rectangular solid is 12 feet, the width is 9 feet, and the volume is 1080 cubic feet. What is the height of the rectangular solid? **(A)**
A) 10 feet   B) 12 feet   C) 90 feet   D) 100 feet

To calculate the volume of a rectangular solid or box, use this formula: *length × width × height*. You are doing the formula in reverse, so you need to divide by 12 and then divide that result by 9 to solve.

72) A beaker is cylindrical and measures 18 inches high and 12 inches in diameter. However, the volume has to be converted from cubic inches to gallons for a report. What is the approximate volume of the beaker in terms of gallons? **(A)**
A) 2.9 gallons   B) 8.8 gallons   C) 10.4 gallons   D) 8,138.88 gallons

The formula for the volume of a cylinder is: volume ≈ 3.14 × (*radius*)² × *height*. To convert cubic inches to gallons: 1 gallon = 231 cubic inches

73) The volume of a cube-shaped object needs to be calculated. The cube has a side length of 9 feet. However, a report is asking for the volume of the object in terms of cubic inches. Which figure below should be used? **(A)**
A) 729 cubic inches
B) 1,728 cubic inches
C) 139,968 cubic inches
D) 1,259,712 cubic inches

The volume of a cube = (*length of side*)^3. 1 cubic foot = 1.728 cubic inches

74) A company ships products overseas in large rectangular shipping containers. One type of container is 25 feet long, 12 feet wide, and 18 feet high. The container is currently 75% full of a particular product. What is the volume in cubic yards of the product in the container? **(A)**
A) 150 cubic yards
B) 200 cubic yards
C) 405 cubic yards
D) 4,050 cubic yards

Use the formula for calculating the volume of a rectangular solid. Your result will be in cubic feet. Then convert to cubic yards to solve. (1 cubic yard = 27 cubic feet)

75) A company manufactures glue and other adhesives that contain a chemical called PVA. At least 50 quarts of PVA need to be in stock at the start of every month. Inventory has been taken this morning and there are 2 containers of PVA that hold 16 cups and 7 ounces each. There are also 3 containers of PVA that hold 20 cups and 4 ounces each. This PVA must be purchased in 5-quart containers. How many containers are needed in order to replenish the stock? **(A)**
A) 0
B) 5
C) 6
D) 7

If you do not know the relationships between ounces and cups, and between cups and quarts, please look at the formula sheet in the appendix.

76) A company that manufactures hand soap and laundry detergent has to order liquid parabens that are used in its products. The parabens are stored in two identically sized vats. The vats measure 10 feet by 10 feet by 12 feet. The first vat is $^3/_4$ full and the second vat is $^4/_5$ full. The parabens cost 12 cents a cubic inch. To the nearest dollar, what is the cost value of the parabens in the two vats? **(A)**
A) $223
B) $3,857
C) $4,977
D) $385,690

Use the formula for calculating the volume of a rectangular solid. Your result will be in cubic feet. Then convert to cubic inches to solve. (1 cubic foot = 1,728 cubic inches)

77) A company that manufactures batteries stores acid in a conical-shaped container that is 6 feet in diameter and 8 feet in height. The manager has calculated that the inside of the container at its maximum could contain approximately 226 cubic feet of acid. What error, if any, has been made in this calculation? **(A)**
A) There is no error in the calculation.
B) The manager forgot to divide by 3.
C) The manager forgot to multiply by 3.14.
D) The manager squared the container's diameter instead of its radius.

Perform the calculations in answers B, C, and D to isolate the error and solve.

78) An electrician installs wiring and lighting in new homes. The client would like to install lights on the walls in the living room. The living room is 25 feet long and 10 feet wide. The client would like a light to be installed on each wall in 5-foot increments. However, no lights are to be installed in the corners of the room. How many lights will be needed in order to carry out this job? **(A)**
A) 8 B) 10 C) 12 D) 14

This is a question on increments in perimeter. You should draw a diagram on your scratch paper to help you answer.

79) A company that manufactures ice cubes and frozen refreshments makes two sizes of ice cubes. The large ice cubes have a side length of 1.8 millimeters, and the small ice cubes have a side length of 1.4 millimeters. What is the amount in cubic millimeters of the difference in volume between the large ice cube and the small one? **(A)**
A) 0.064 B) 1.960 C) 2.744 D) 3.088

Calculate the volume of each cube. Then subtract these two results to solve. Remember that the volume of a cube = (*length of side*)^3.

80) A building engineer has been asked to calculate the areas of two triangular shapes. The large triangle has a base of 12 inches and a height of 18 inches. The small triangle has a base of 8 inches and a height of 14 inches. What is the difference in the areas of the two shapes? **(D)**
A) 8 B) 16 C) 25 D) 52

Use the formula for the area of a triangle that we have seen in a previous question in this section. Then subtract to solve.

Data Analysis, Statistics & Probability

81) A student receives the following scores on his exams during the semester: 89, 65, 75, 68, 82, 74, 86. What is the mean of his scores? **(D)**

A) 24 B) 74 C) 75 D) 77

The arithmetic mean is the same thing as the arithmetic average. In order to calculate the mean, add up the values of all of the items in the set, and then divide by the number of items in the set.

82) Members of a weight loss group report their individual weight loss to the group leader every week. During the week, the following amounts in pounds were reported: 1, 1, 3, 2, 4, 3, 1, 2, and 1. What is the mode of the weight loss for the group? **(D)**
A) 1 pound B) 2 pounds C) 3 pounds D) 4 pounds

This is a question on mode. Mode is the value that occurs most frequently in a data set. For example, if 10 students scored 85 on a test, 6 students scored 90, and 4 students scored 80, the mode score is 85.

83) Mark's record of times for the 400 meter freestyle at swim meets this season is: 8.19, 7.59, 8.25, 7.35, and 9.10. What is the median of his times? **(D)**
A) 7.59 B) 8.19 C) 8.25 D) 8.096

84) Find the median of the following data set: 10, 12, 8, 2, 5, 21, 8, 6, 2, 3 **(D)**

A) 7   B) 6.5   C) 2   D) 19

> These two questions are asking you to find the median of a set of numbers. If there is an odd number of items in the data set, the median is the number that is in the middle of the set when the numbers are in ascending order. If there is an even number of items in the data set, we have to take the average of the two numbers that are in the middle of the set when the numbers have been placed in ascending order.

85) A student receives the following scores on her assignments during the term: 98.5, 85.5, 80.0, 97, 93, 92.5, 93, 87, 88, 82. What is the range of her scores? **(D)**

A) 17.0   B) 18.0   C) 18.5   D) 89.65

> This is a question on calculating range. To calculate range, the lowest value in the data set is deducted from the highest value in the data set.

86) What is the mode of the numbers in the following list? 1.6, 2.9, 4.5, 2.5, 5.1, 5.4 **(A)**

A) 3.5   B) 3.1   C) 3.0   D) no mode

> This is another question on mode. What happens to the mode if no number in the set occurs more than once?

87) There are 10 cars in a parking lot. Nine of the cars are 2, 3, 4, 5, 6, 7, 9, 10, and 12 years old, respectively. If the average age of the 10 cars is 6 years old, how old is the 10th car? **(A)**

A) 1 year old   B) 2 years old   C) 3 years old   D) 4 years old

> This is a question on how to calculate the missing value from the calculation of the mean. We don't know the age of the 10th car, so set up an equation and put this in as x to solve:
> $(2 + 3 + 4 + 5 + 6 + 7 + 9 + 10 + 12 + x) \div 10 = 6$

88) 100 participants took an intelligence test. The mean score for the first 50 participants was 82, and the mean score for the next 50 participants was 89. What is the mean test score for all 100 participants? **(A)**

A) 85.5   B) 86.5   C) 87   D) 88

> Find the total points for the first group. Then find the total points for the second group. Add these two results together to find the total points for all the participants. Then divide the total points by the total number of members in the group.

89) An employee at the Department of Motor Vehicles wanted to find the mean of the ten driving theory tests he administered this morning. However, the employee divided the total points from the ten tests by 8, which gave him an erroneous result of 78. What is the correct mean of the ten tests? **(A)**

A) 97.5   B) 70   C) 62.4   D) 52

> Multiply 78 by 8 to get the total points. Then divide by 10 to solve.

90) A bag contains 5 red balloons, 10 orange balloons, 8 green balloons, and 12 purple balloons. If a balloon is drawn from the bag at random, what is the probability that it will be orange? **(A)**

A) $\dfrac{2}{7}$ B) $\dfrac{1}{4}$ C) $\dfrac{1}{10}$ D) $\dfrac{1}{35}$

This is a question on calculating basic probability. First of all, calculate how many items there are in total in the data set, which is also called the "sample space" or (S). Then reduce the data set if further items are removed. Probability can be expressed as a fraction. The number of items available in the total data set goes in the denominator. The chance of the desired outcome, which is also referred to as the event or (E), goes in the numerator of the fraction. You can determine the chance of the event by calculating how many items are available for the desired outcome.

91) A deck of cards contains 13 hearts, 13 diamonds, 13 clubs, and 13 spades. Cards are selected from the deck at random. Once selected, the cards are discarded and are not placed back into the deck. Two spades, one heart, and a club are drawn from the deck. What is the probability that the next card drawn from the deck will be a heart? **(A)**

A) $1/13$ B) $1/12$ C) $13/52$ D) $1/4$

Reduce the sample space by the number of cards that have already been drawn for the denominator. Then determine how many hearts are left for the numerator.

92) Sam rolls a fair pair of six-sided dice. One of the die is black and the other is red. Each die has values from 1 to 6. What is the probability that Sam will roll a 4 on the red die and a 5 on the black die? **(A)**

A) $1/36$ B) $2/36$ C) $1/12$ D) $2/12$

Determine how many combinations are possible on a set of dice. You may want to write down the possible combinations, which will make the answer clearer to you.

93) An owner of a carnival attraction draws teddy bears out of a bag at random to give to prize winners. She has 10 brown teddy bears, 8 white teddy bears, 4 black teddy bears, and 2 pink teddy bears when she opens the attraction at the start of the day. The first prize winner of the day receives a brown teddy bear. What is the probability that the second prize winner will receive a pink teddy bear? **(A)**

A) $1/24$ B) $1/23$ C) $2/24$ D) $2/23$

For the denominator, reduce the sample space by the number of bears that have already been drawn. Then determine how many pink teddy bears are left for the numerator.

For questions 94 to 100, study the charts carefully, paying attention to the legends and labels on each one. Read each question carefully to be sure what calculation you need to do. Then perform the operations to solve.

Look at the bar chart below and answer questions 94 to 97.

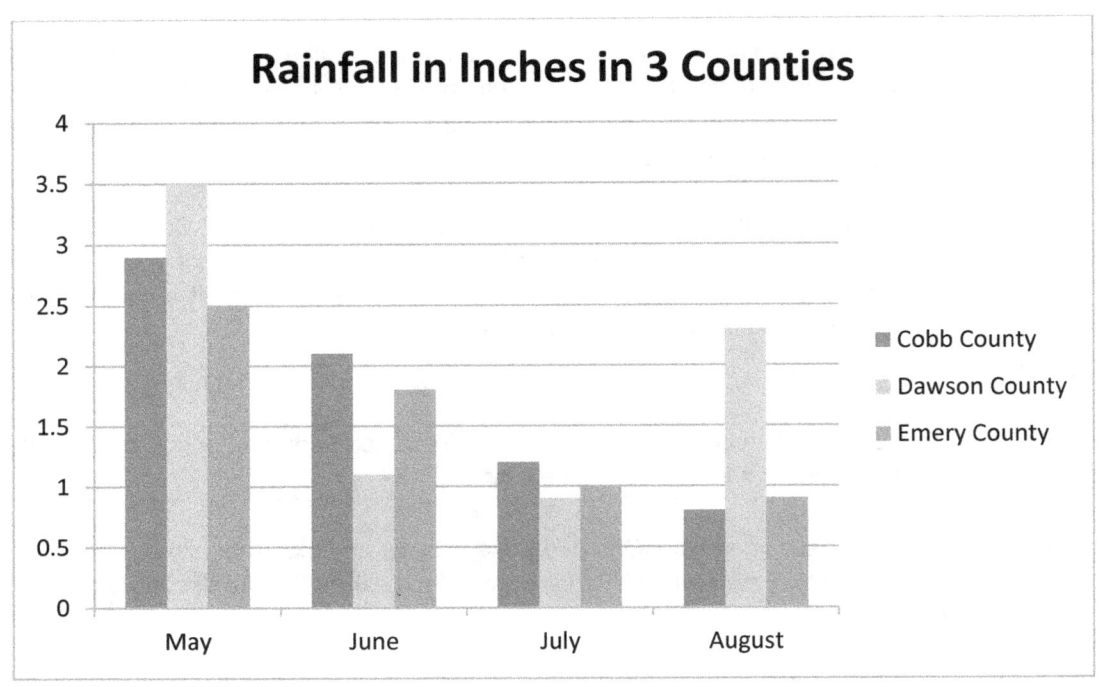

94) Approximately how many inches of rainfall did Cobb County have for July and August in total? **(D)**
A) 0.7 inches B) 0.9 inches C) 2 inches D) 3.2 inches

95) What was the approximate difference in the amount of rainfall for Dawson County and Emery County for June? **(D)**
A) Dawson County had 0.6 more inches of rainfall than Emery County.
B) Emery County had 0.6 more inches of rainfall than Dawson County.
C) Dawson County had 1.1 fewer inches of rainfall than Emery County.
D) Emery County had 1.1 fewer inches of rainfall than Dawson County.

96) What was the approximate total rainfall for Emery County for all four months? **(D)**
A) 6.2 inches B) 6.8 inches C) 7.0 inches D) 7.4 inches

97) Which figure below best represents the total amount of rainfall in inches for the county that had the least amount of rainfall for all four months in total? **(D)**
A) 6.2 B) 6.9 C) 7 D) 7.8

Look at the pie chart and information below and answer questions 98 to 100.

A zoo has reptiles, birds, quadrupeds, and fish. At the start of the year, they have a total of 1,500 creatures living in the zoo. The pie chart below shows percentages by category for the 1,500 creatures at the start of the year. At the end of the year, the zoo still has 1,500 creatures, but reptiles constitute 40%, quadrupeds 21%, and fish 16%.

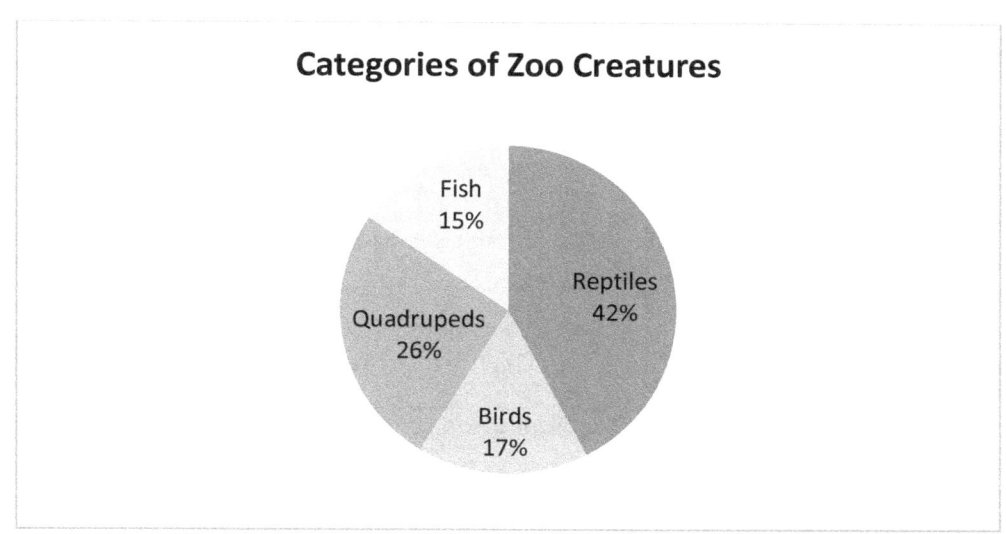

98) How many reptiles are in the zoo at the start of the year? **(M)**
A) 225 B) 255 C) 390 D) 630

99) What was the difference between the number of quadrupeds at the start of the year and the number of fish at the start of the year? **(D)**
A) There were 165 more fish than quadrupeds.
B) There were 165 more quadrupeds than fish.
C) There were 75 more fish than quadrupeds.
D) There were 75 more quadrupeds than fish.

100) What can be said about the number of birds at the end of the year when compared to the number of birds at the beginning of the year? **(D)**
A) There were 23 more birds at the end of the year than at the beginning of the year.
B) There were 23 fewer birds at the end of the year than at the beginning of the year.
C) There were 90 more birds at the end of the year than at the beginning of the year.
D) There were 90 fewer birds at the end of the year than at the beginning of the year.

Algebra, Functions, and Patterns

Expressions with One Variable

101) Evaluate: $2x^2 - x + 5$ if $x = -2$ **(D)**
 A) 2 B) 7 C) 15 D) 17

Step 1 – To perform the operations on the first term of the equation, multiply –2 by itself to square it. Then multiply this result by 2. Step 2 – To get your final answer, take the result from step 1 and subtract –2 and add 5.

102) Solve for x: $-6x + 5 = -19$ **(D)**
 A) 2 B) 4 C) 6 D) 8

Isolate x to one side of the equation by subtracting 5 from both sides of the equation. Then multiply each side of the new equation by –6 to isolate x and solve.

103) If $4x - 3(x + 2) = -3$, then $x = ?$ **(D)**
 A) 9 B) 3 C) 1 D) –3

Multiply the terms inside the parentheses by the –3 in front of the set of parentheses. Then simplify and isolate x to one side of the equation to solve.

104) If $\frac{3}{4}x - 2 = 4$, $x = ?$ **(D)**
 A) $\frac{8}{3}$ B) $\frac{1}{8}$ C) 8 D) –8

Multiply each side of the equation by $\frac{4}{3}$ to get rid of the fraction. Then simplify the remaining new improper fraction and add the result of the simplified fraction to both sides of the equation solve.

105) What is the value of $\frac{x-3}{2-x}$ when $x = 1$? **(D)**
 A) 2 B) –2 C) ½ D) –½

Substitute 1 for the value of x. Then perform the subtraction in the numerator and the subtraction in the dominator. Then simplify the resulting fraction to solve.

Expressions with Two Variables

106) $x^2 + xy - y = 41$ and $x = 5$. What is the value of y? **(D)**
 A) 2.6 B) 4 C) 6 D) –4

107) $x^2 + xy - y = 254$ and $x = 12$. What is the value of y? **(D)**
 A) 110 B) 10 C) 11 D) 12

For the two above questions, substitute the stated values of x. Then perform the necessary operations on both sides of the equation to isolate y and solve.

Roots and Radicals

108) If $6 + 8(2\sqrt{x} + 4) = 62$, then $\sqrt{x}$ = ? **(D)**
 A) 3.25
 B) 24
 C) $\frac{3}{2}$
 D) $\frac{2}{3}$

Perform the multiplication on the parenthetical first. The get rid of the integers by subtracting them from both sides of the equations. Then divide by 16 to isolate $\sqrt{x}$ to solve.

109) Which of the answers below is equal to the following radical expression? $\sqrt{50}$ **(D)**
 A) $1 \div 50$
 B) $2\sqrt{25}$
 C) $2\sqrt{5}$
 D) $5\sqrt{2}$

Step 1 – Factor the number inside the square root sign. Step 2 – Look to see if any of the factors are perfect squares. In this case, the only factor that is a perfect square is 25. Step 3 – Find the square root of 25 then simplify.

110) $\sqrt{36} + 4\sqrt{72} - 2\sqrt{144}$ = ? **(D)**
 A) $2\sqrt{36}$
 B) $2\sqrt{252}$
 C) $18 + 24\sqrt{2}$
 D) $-18 + 24\sqrt{2}$

Step 1 – Find the common factors that are perfect squares. Step 2 – Factor the amounts inside each of the radical signs and simplify.

111) $\sqrt{7} \times \sqrt{11}$ = ? **(D)**
 A) $\sqrt{77}$
 B) $\sqrt{18}$
 C) $7\sqrt{11}$
 D) $11\sqrt{7}$

Step 1 – Multiply the numbers inside the radical signs. Step 2 – Put this product inside a radical symbol for your answer.

112) Simplify: $\sqrt{15} + 3\sqrt{15}$ **(A)**
 A) 45
 B) $4\sqrt{15}$
 C) $2\sqrt{15}$
 D) $3\sqrt{30}$

You can place the number 1 in front of the first radical because it will count only one time. Then add the numbers in front of the radical signs to solve.

113) Express as a rational number: $\sqrt[3]{\frac{216}{27}}$ **(A)**
 A) 3
 B) 2
 C) $\frac{7}{3}$
 D) $\sqrt[3]{2}$

Step 1 – Find the cube roots of the numerator and denominator to eliminate the radical. Step 2 – Simplify further if possible. The cube root is a number that equals the required product when multiplied by itself two times.

Exponent Laws

114) $7^5 \times 7^3 = ?$ **(D)**

A) 7^8 B) 7^{15} C) 14^8 D) 49^8

> If the base number is the same, you need to add the exponents when multiplying, but keep the base number the same as before.

115) $xy^6 \div xy^3 = ?$ **(A)**

A) xy^{18} B) xy^3 C) x^2y^3 D) xy^2

> If the base number is the same, you need to subtract the exponents when dividing, but keep the base number the same as before.

116) $\sqrt{8x^4} \cdot \sqrt{32x^6} = ?$ **(A)**

A) $8\sqrt{32x^{10}}$ B) $16x^{10}$ C) $16x^5$ D) $256x^{10}$

> This question combines the laws or radicals with the laws of exponents.

117) A rocket flies at a speed of 1.7×10^5 miles per hour for 2×10^{-1} hours. How far has this rocket gone? **(A)**

A) 340,000 miles   B) 34,000 miles   C) 3,400 miles   D) 340 miles

> Step 1: Add the exponents to multiply the 10's. Step 2: Multiply the miles per hour by the number of hours to get the distance traveled. Step 3: Then multiply these two results together to solve the problem.

118) $\sqrt{x^{\frac{5}{7}}} = ?$ **(A)**

A) $\dfrac{5x}{7}$ B) $\left(\sqrt[5]{x}\right)^7$ C) $\left(7\sqrt{x}\right)^5$ D) $\left(\sqrt[7]{x}\right)^5$

> Step 1: Put the base number inside the radical sign. Step 2: The denominator of the exponent is the nth root of the radical. Step 3: The numerator is the new exponent.

119) $x^{-5} = ?$ **(A)**

A) $\dfrac{1}{x^{-5}}$ B) $\dfrac{1}{x^5}$ C) $-5x$ D) $\dfrac{1}{5x}$

120) $(-4)^{-3} = ?$ **(A)**

A) -64 B) $-\dfrac{1}{64}$ C) $\dfrac{1}{64}$ D) 64

> Step 1: When you have an exponent that is a negative number, you need to set up a fraction, where 1 is the numerator. Step 2: Put the term with the exponent in the denominator, but remove the negative sign on the exponent.

121) $62^0 = ?$ **(A)**

　A) −62　　　B) 0　　　C) 1　　　D) 62

122) $(25x)^0 = ?$ **(A)**

　A) 0　　　B) 5　　　C) 1　　　D) 25

> Any non-zero number raised to the power of zero is equal to 1.

Simplifying Rational Algebraic Expressions

123) $\dfrac{b + \frac{2}{7}}{\frac{1}{b}} = ?$ **(A)**

　A) $b^2 + \dfrac{7}{2}$　　B) $2b + \dfrac{7}{2}$　　C) $b^2 + \dfrac{2b}{7}$　　D) $\dfrac{b}{b + \frac{2}{7}}$

> Step 1 – When the expression has fractions in both the numerator and denominator, treat the line in the main fraction as the division symbol. Step 2 – Invert the fraction that was in the denominator and multiply.

124) $\dfrac{x^2}{x^2 + 2x} + \dfrac{8}{x} = ?$ **(A)**

　A) $\dfrac{x + 8x + 16}{x^2 + 2x}$　　B) $\dfrac{x^2 + 8}{x^2 + 3x}$　　C) $\dfrac{8x^2 + 16x}{x^3}$　　D) $\dfrac{x^2 + 8x + 16}{x^2 + 2x}$

> Step 1 – Find the lowest common denominator. Since x is common to both denominators, we can convert the denominator of the second fraction to the LCD by multiplying the numerator and denominator of the second fraction by $(x + 2)$. Step 2 – When both fractions have the LCD, add the numerators to solve.

125) Perform the operation and simplify: $\dfrac{2a^3}{7} \times \dfrac{3}{a^2} = ?$ **(A)**

　A) $\dfrac{6a}{7}$　　B) $\dfrac{5a^3}{7a^2}$　　C) $\dfrac{2a^6}{21}$　　D) $\dfrac{21}{2a^6}$

> Step 1 – Multiply the numerator of the first fraction by the numerator of the second fraction to get the new numerator. Step 2 – Then multiply the denominators. Step 3 – Factor out a^2. Step 4 – Simplify.

126) $\dfrac{8x + 8}{x^4} \div \dfrac{5x + 5}{x^2} = ?$ **(A)**

　A) $\dfrac{5x^2}{8}$　　B) $\dfrac{8}{5x^2}$　　C) $\dfrac{3x+3}{x^2}$　　D) $\dfrac{x^2 + 8x + 8}{x^4 + 5x + 5}$

> Step 1 – Invert and multiply by the second fraction. Step 2 – Cancel out $(x + 1)$. Step 3 – Cancel out x^2.

Factoring Polynomials

127) Factor: $9x^3 - 3x$ **(D)**
   A) $3x(3x^2 - 1)$
   B) $3x(3x - 1)$
   C) $3x(x^2 - 1)$
   D) $3x(x - 3)$

128) Which of the following is a factor of: $2xy - 6x^2y + 4x^2y^2$ **(D)**
   A) $(1 + 3x - 2xy)$
   B) $(1 - 3x + 2xy)$
   C) $(1 + 3x + 2xy)$
   D) $(1 - 3x - 2xy)$

> To factor an equation, you need to find the common factor for all of the terms in the equation. So, for the first question above, you need to divide all of the terms by $3x$. For the second question above, you need to divide all of the terms by $2xy$.

Equivalent Expressions

129) Which of the following mathematical expressions equals $3/xy$? **(D)**
   A) $3/x \times 3/y$
   B) $3 \div 3xy$
   C) $3 \div (xy)$
   D) $1/3 \div 3xy$

> To find the equivalent expression, remember that the line in a fraction can be treated as the division symbol.

130) Which of the following is equivalent to the expression $2(x + 2)(x - 3)$ for all values of x? **(D)**
   A) $2x^2 - 2x - 12$
   B) $2x^2 - 10x - 6$
   C) $2x^2 + 2x - 12$
   D) $2x^2 + 10x - 6$

> Perform the FOIL method on the parentheticals. Then multiply this result by 2 to solve. If you do not know how to perform the FOIL method, you may want to look at questions 132 and 133 first.

131) Which of the following is equivalent to $\frac{x}{5} \div \frac{9}{y}$? **(A)**

   A) $\frac{xy}{45}$
   B) $\frac{9x}{5y}$
   C) $\frac{1}{9} \times \frac{x}{5y}$
   D) $\frac{1}{5} \times \frac{9}{5y}$

> Remember that to divide by a fraction, you need to invert the second fraction and the multiply.

Expanding Polynomials

132) Which of the following expressions is equivalent to $(x + 4y)^2$? **(D)**
   A) $2(x + 8y)$
   B) $2x + 8y$
   C) $x^2 + 8xy^2 + 16y^2$
   D) $x^2 + 8xy + 16y^2$

133) $(2 + \sqrt{6})^2 = ?$ **(D)**
   A) 8
   B) $8 + 2\sqrt{6}$
   C) $8 + 4\sqrt{6}$
   D) $10 + 4\sqrt{6}$

> When expanding polynomials, you should use the FOIL method: First – Outside – Inside – Last. We can demonstrate the FOIL method on an example equation as follows:
> $(a + b)(c + d) =$
> $(a \times c) + (a \times d) + (b \times c) + (b \times d) =$
> $ac + ad + bc + bd$

Linear Equations

134) A mother has noticed that the more sugar her child eats, the more her child sleeps at night. Which of the following graphs best illustrates the relationship between the amount of sugar the child consumes and the child's amount of sleep? **(D)**

A)

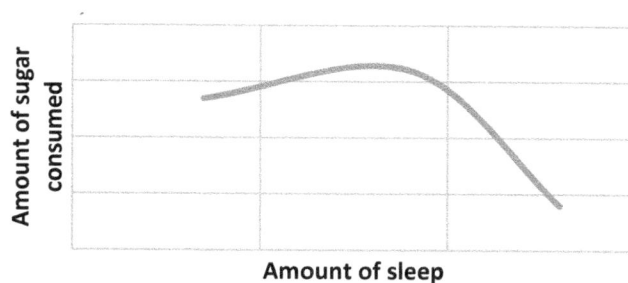

B)

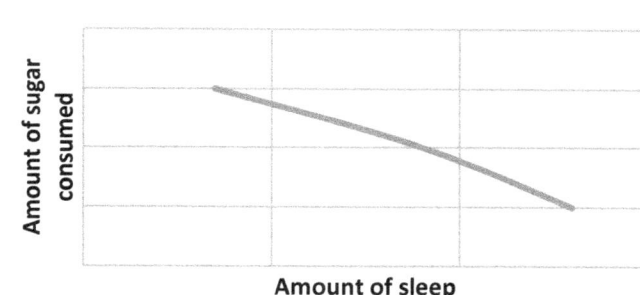

C)

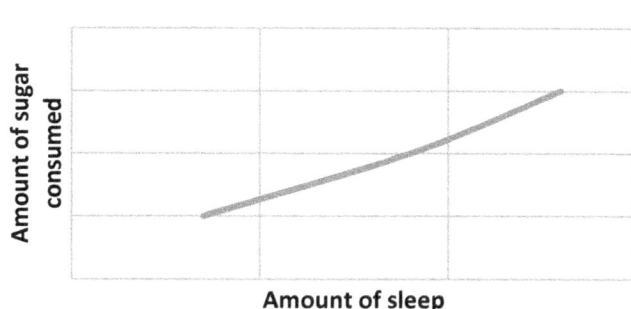

D)

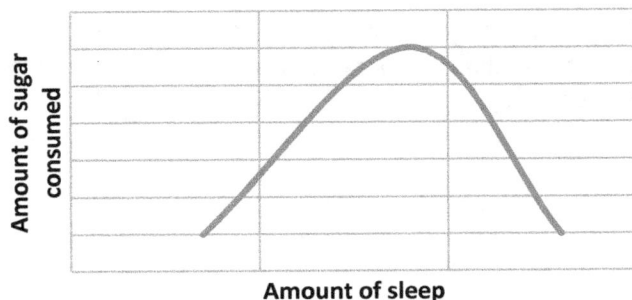

Amount of sleep

> You will need to know the difference between positive linear relationships and negative linear relationships for the exam. In a positive linear relationship, an increase in one variable causes an increase in the other variable, meaning that the line will point upwards from left to right.
>
> In a negative linear relationship, an increase in one variable causes a decrease in the other variable, meaning that the line will point downwards from left to right.

Algebraic Functions

135) The graph of a linear equation is shown below. Which one of the tables of values best represents the points on the graph? **(D)**

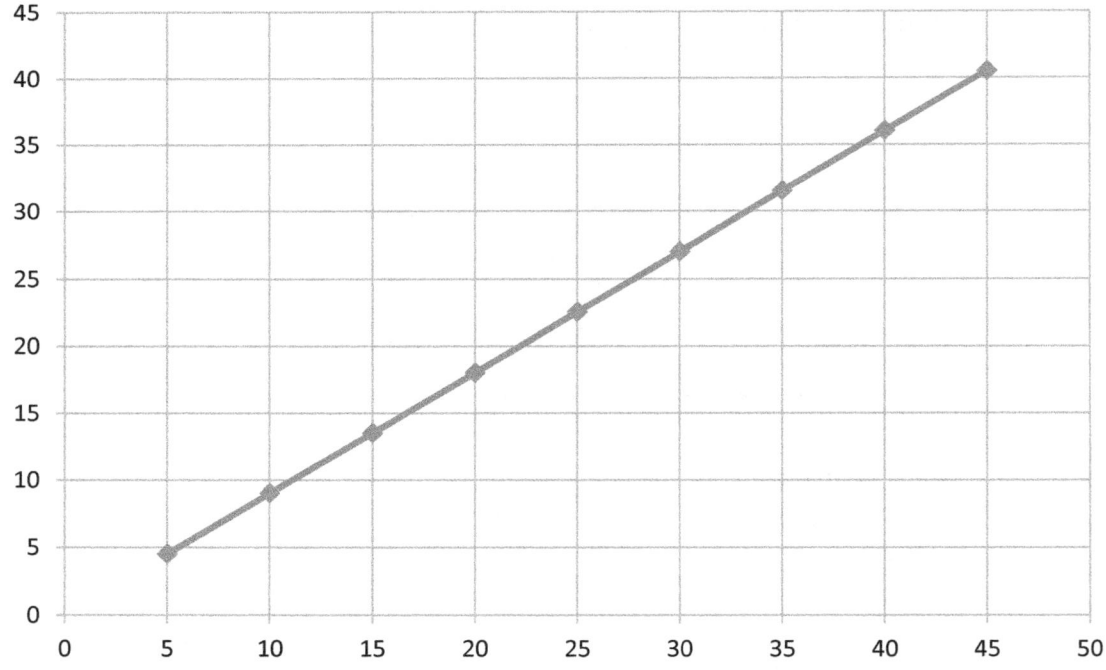

A)

x	y
5	5
10	10
15	15
20	20

B)

x	y
5	4
10	8
15	12
20	16

C)

x	y
5	4.5
10	9
15	13.5
20	18

D)

x	y
5	9
10	13
15	15
20	20

This is an example of an exam question involving algebraic functions. A function expresses the mathematical relationship between x and y. So, a certain recurring mathematical operation on x will yield the output of y. Step 1: Look carefully at the point that is furthest to the left on the graph. You will be able to eliminate several of the answer choices because they will not state this first coordinate correctly.
Step 2: Try to work out the relationship between the coordinates of the first point to those of the next point on the line. Use the horizontal and vertical grid lines on the graph to help you.

136) What is the value of $f_1(2)$ where $f_1(x) = 5^x$? **(A)**

A) 2^5 B) 10   C) 25   D) 25^2

For this type of algebraic function, substitute the value of 2 for x in the second expression.

137) For the two functions $f_1(x)$ and $f_2(x)$, tables of vales are given below. What is the value of $f_2(f_1(2))$? **(A)**

x	$f_1(x)$
1	3
2	5
3	7
4	9
5	11

x	$f_2(x)$
2	4
3	9
4	16
5	25
6	36

A) 4
B) 5
C) 9
D) 25

Solve the first function for the value of 2. The take the resulting number and put it in as the value of x in the second function.

138) For the functions $f_2(x)$ listed below, x and y are integers greater than 1. If $f_1(x) = x^2$, which of the functions below has the greatest value for $f_1(f_2(x))$? **(A)**
A) $f_2(x) = x/y$ B) $f_2(x) = y/x$ C) $f_2(x) = xy$ D) $f_2(x) = x - y$

Look at all of the answer choices, and substitute any positive integers for x and y. Then try the same using negative integers.

139) If $f(x) = x^2 + 3x - 8$, what is $f(x+3)$? **(A)**
A) $(x+3)^2 + 3x - 8$
B) $(x+3)^2 + 3(x+3) - 8$
C) $x^2 + 3x - 5$
D) $3(x^2 + 3x - 8)$

Substitute x + 3 for x to solve.

Logarithmic Functions

140) If $\log_3(x+2) = 4$, then $x = $? **(A)**
A) 66
B) 79
C) 81
D) 83

To convert a logarithmic function to an exponent, the number after the equals sign (4 in this problem) becomes the exponent. The small subscript number after "log" (3 in this problem) becomes the base number. Then perform the multiplication to solve.

Quadratic Equations

141) Simplify: $(x - y)(x + y)$ **(A)**
   A) $x^2 - 2xy - y^2$ B) $x^2 + 2xy - y^2$ C) $x^2 + y^2$ D) $x^2 - y^2$

Use the FOIL method on quadratic equations like this one when the instructions tell you to simplify. If you do not remember how to perform the FOIL method, look at questions 132 and 133 again. Then try the next question.

142) $(3x + y)(x - 5y) = ?$ **(A)**
   A) $3x^2 - 14xy - 5y^2$
   B) $3x^2 - 14xy + 5y^2$
   C) $3x^2 + 14xy - 5y^2$
   D) $3x^2 + 14xy + 5y^2$

Linear Inequalities

143) $50 - \dfrac{3x}{5} \geq 41$, then $x \leq ?$ **(D)**
   A) 15   B) 25   C) 41   D) 50

Step 1: Isolate the whole numbers to one side of the inequality. Step 2: Get rid of the fraction by multiplying each side by 5. Step 3: Divide to simplify further. Step 4: Isolate the variable to solve.

144) The cost of one wizfit is equal to y. If $x - 2 > 5$ and $y = x - 2$, then the cost of 2 wizfits is greater than which one of the following? **(D)**
   A) $x - 2$ B) $x - 5$ C) $y + 5$ D) 10

Look to see if the inequality and the equation have any variables or terms in common. In this problem, both the inequality and the equation contain $x - 2$. The cost of one wizfit is represented by y, and y is equal to $x - 2$. So, we can substitute values from the equation to the inequality.

Quadratic Inequalities

145) Solve for x: $x^2 - 9 < 0$ **(A)**
   A) $x < -3$ or $x > 3$
   B) $x > -3$ or $x < 3$
   C) $x < -3$ or $x < 3$
   D) $x > -3$ or $x > 3$

For quadratic inequality problems like this one, you need to factor the inequality first. We know that the factors of -9 are: -1×9; -3×3; 1×-9. We do not have a term with only the x variable, so we need factors that add up to zero. $-3 + 3 = 0$. So, try to solve the problem based on these facts. Be sure to check your answer by substituting greater or lesser values (like 4 and -4) into the original inequality.

146) Solve for x: $x^2 - 5x + 6 \leq 0$ **(A)**
   A) $2 \geq x \geq 3$
   B) $2 \leq x \leq 3$
   C) $x < -3$ or $x < 2$
   D) $x > -2$ or $x > 3$

Here is another quadratic inequality problem. Remember to factor the inequality first. We know that the factors of 6 are: 1×6 and 2×3. We have a term with the x variable, so we need factors that add up to five. $2 + 3 = 5$. So, try to solve the problem based on these facts. Be sure to check your work to be sure the signs point the right way by substituting values into the original inequality.

Systems of Equations

147) What ordered pair is a solution to the following system of equations? **(A)**
$x + y = 7$
$xy = 12$

A) (2, 6) B) (6, 2) C) (4, 2) D) (3, 4)

> Step 1: Look at the multiplication equation and find the factors of 12. Step 2: Add the factors in each set together to see if they equal 7 to solve the addition in the first equation.

148) Solve by elimination: $3x + 3y = 15$ and $x + 2y = 8$ **(A)**

A) $x = -18$ and $y = 13$
B) $x = -2$ and $y = 3$
C) $x = 2$ and $y = 3$
D) $x = 3$ and $y = 2$

> Step 1: Look at the x term of the first equation, which is 3x. In order to eliminate the x variable, we need to multiply the second equation by 3. Step 2: Subtract this result from the first equation to solve.

Patterns

Sequences and Series – Arithmetic Sequences and Series

149) What is the next number in the following sequence? 1, 5, 9, 13, 17, . . . **(M)**

A) 20 B) 21 C) 30 D) 40

> Sequences are numbers in a list like the following: 1, 3, 5, 7, 9. In a series, the numbers are added: 1 + 3 + 5 + 7 + 9. In an arithmetic sequence, the difference between one number and the next is known as a constant. In other words, you add the same value each time until you reach the end of the sequence. The formula for the nth number of an arithmetic sequence is a + [d × (n – 1)], where variable *a* represents the starting number and variable *d* represents the difference or constant.

Sequences and Series – Geometric Sequences and Series

150) What is the next number in the following sequence? 2, 6, 18, 54, . . . **(D)**

A) 60 B) 72 C) 80 D) 162

> When the sequence cannot be solved by addition, then you usually have a geometric sequence.
> In a geometric sequence, each number is found by multiplying the previous term by a factor known as a common ratio. Where the first number is represented by variable *a* and the factor (called the "common ratio") is represented by variable *r*, the formula for calculating the nth item in a geometric sequence is: $ar^{(n-1)}$

TABE 9 & 10 Practice Test 1

151) An online magazine business charges a $59 subscription fee for every customer who signs up during the week. This week, 14 customers signed up. How much did the business make on upfront subscription fees for these customers this week? **(E)**
A) $726
B) $762
C) $826
D) $862

152) Packaging weight changes for the first three years of business were as follows. Year 1: –92 grams; Year 2: 35 grams; Year 3: –16 grams. What figure below represents the change in the packaging weight from year 1 to year 2? **(E)**
A) –57
B) 57
C) 19
D) 127

153) A business's expenses for the first three years were as follows: $12,225; $43,871; and $69,423. What were the total expenses for the first three years of business? **(E)**
A) $125,339
B) $125,465
C) $125,519
D) $125,528

154) A customer handed the cashier $75 to pay for the items she purchased, and the cashier gave her the correct change of $8.35. What was the total cost of the items the customer purchased? **(E)**
A) $66.65
B) $66.75
C) $65.65
D) $66.55

155) Stock option investments can go up or down in value each day. Investment gains are represented as positive numbers, and investment losses are represented as negative numbers. At the end of one particular day, the gains and losses for five investments were as follows: –205, 39, –107, 18, 126. What was the total investment gain for loss for all five investments for this day? **(E)**
A) 85
B) 129
C) –129
D) –192

156) An auto shop does custom paint and vinyl wrap jobs on vintage cars. An employee worked 7.5 hours each day for 2 days on a job for one customer. The customer was billed $75 per hour for the employee's work, and the employee was paid $40 per hour. How much money did the shop make for the work on this job after paying the employee's wages? **(M)**
A) $262.50
B) $300.00
C) $525.00
D) $600.00

157) A liquid ingredient is stored in 5-quart containers. There are two partially-full containers, one with $4^{3}/_{8}$ quarts and another with $3^{7}/_{8}$ quarts. How many quarts are there in total in these two containers? **(M)**
   A) $1^{1}/_{4}$
   B) 7
   C) $7^{1}/_{8}$
   D) $8^{1}/_{4}$

158) A small factory uses tarpaulin to make covers for farm implements. There was $12^{7}/_{16}$ yards of tarpaulin at the start of the day. At the end of the day, $8^{9}/_{16}$ yards of tarpaulin is left. Which amount below represents the amount of tarpaulin used this day in yards? **(M)**
   A) $2^{14}/_{16}$
   B) $3^{1}/_{8}$
   C) $3^{7}/_{8}$
   D) $4^{7}/_{8}$

159) Abdul purchased 80 items for sale, and he has sold 0.75 of them in relation to the total purchased. How many items does he have left after making these sales? **(M)**
   A) 10 items
   B) 20 items
   C) 25 items
   D) 40 items

160) A class has n students. In this class, t% of the students subscribe to digital TV packages. Which of the following represents the number of students who do not subscribe to any digital TV package? **(M)**
   A) $100(n - t)$
   B) $(100\% - t\%) \times n$
   C) $(100\% - t\%) \div n$
   D) $(1 - t)n$

161) For a particular sugar-craft product, 3 parts of icing sugar must be added to every 6 parts of sugar paste. A batch of sugar-craft that has 14 parts of sugar paste is being prepared. How many parts of icing sugar should be added to this batch? **(M)**
   A) 3
   B) 6
   C) 7
   D) 8

162) In a shipment of 100 mp3 players, 1% of the mp3 players are faulty. What is the ratio of non-faulty mp3 players to faulty mp3 players? **(M)**
   A) 99:1
   B) 1:100
   C) 100:1
   D) 1:99

163) A cell phone is purchased at a cost of x and sold at four times the cost. Which of the following represents the profit on each of these cell phones? **(M)**
   A) x
   B) $3x$
   C) $4x$
   D) $3 - x$

164) An internet provider sells internet packages based on monthly rates. The price (P) for the internet service depends on the speed (s) of the internet connection. The chart that follows indicates the prices of the various internet packages. **(M)**
Price in Dollars: $10 $20 $30 $40
Speed in GB: 2 4 6 8
Which equation represents the prices of these internet packages?
A) $P = (s - 5) \times 5$
B) $P = (s + 5) \times 5$
C) $P = 5 \div s$
D) $P = s \times 5$

165) During the first nine hours of production, the following amounts of units were produced per hour: 1, 2, 3, 4, 5, 5, 8, 8, 9. Which figure below represents the mean production in units per hour for the first nine hours of production? **(D)**
A) 1
B) 2
C) 5
D) 8

166) Seven orders were received yesterday for the following numbers of units: 12, 20, 3, 25, 30, 28, and 18. What was the median number of units ordered yesterday? **(D)**
A) 12
B) 13
C) 20
D) 35

167) J represents jeans and T represents T-shirts in these equations: $2J + T = \$50$ and $J + 2T = \$40$. A customer buys one pair of jeans and one T-shirt. How much does she pay for her entire purchase? **(D)**
A) $10
B) $20
C) $30
D) $40

168) Galvanized pipe is manufactured in 1/64 inch increments in diameter. You have selected a pipe that is 23/64 inch diameter, but have realized that it is too large for your current project. What size diameter should you try next? **(M)**
A) 1/4
B) 11/32
C) 12/32
D) 13/32

169) A footwear store can purchase 325 pairs of tennis shoes from its normal supplier for $4 a pair. It can get the same 325 pairs of shoes from a second supplier for $1,250 plus 6% sales tax, or from a third supplier for $1,290. How much will the store pay to get the best deal? **(M)**
A) $1,250.00
B) $1,290.00
C) $1,300.00
D) $1,367.40

170) A textile manufacturing company can buy cloth for $3 a meter from an overseas supplier. However, the cost of the cloth needs to be reported in inches for the company's financial statements. How many inches of cloth can be purchased for $3? (1 inch = 2.54 centimeters; 1 meter = 100 centimeters) **(M)**
A) 2.54
B) 3.937
C) 39.37
D) 100

171) Angle A of a triangle measures 36°. Angles B and C have the same measurement each in degrees. What is the measurement of angle B? **(D)**
A) 36°
B) 45°
C) 72°
D) 144°

172) A football field is 100 yards long and 30 yards wide. What is the area of the football field in square yards? **(D)**
A) 3000
B) 1500
C) 300
D) 260

173) A small pasture has a length of 5 yards and a width of 3 yards. Barbed wire will be placed on all four sides of the outside of this pasture. How many yards of barbed wire should be ordered? **(D)**
A) 15
B) 16
C) 18
D) 40

174) A circular ornament has a diameter of 12. Which formula should be used to calculate the circumference of the ornament? **(D)**
A) 6 × 3.14
B) 12 × 3.14
C) 24 × 3.14
D) 36 × 3.14

175) A box is manufactured to contain either laptop computers or notebook computers. When the computer systems are removed from the box, it is reused to hold other items. If the length of the box is 20 centimeters (cm), the width is 15cm, and the height is 25cm, what is the volume of the box in cubic centimeters? **(A)**
A) 150
B) 300
C) 750
D) 7500

176) A production line has 6 different production stages that the product must pass through before it is completed. Each production stage lasts for 9 seconds, and the set-up time for each stage is an additional 2 seconds. The production line shift begins at 6:00 AM and a count of items produced takes place every 10 minutes, with the first count to take place at 6:10 AM. The items are counted after they are placed into a box, and there is a further 5 second packaging time for each box that is filled. How many items will have been packaged in the box when the first count is taken at 6:10 AM? **(A)**
A) 0
B) 6

C) 9
D) 37

177) An individual tire-and-rim product weighs 32 pounds and 4 ounces. The product is loaded into a wooden crate, and the crate when empty weighs 60 pounds. Each individual rim weighs 19 pounds. The crate when completely full to capacity weighs 447 pounds. How many units can each crate contain? **(A)**
A) 11
B) 12
C) 13
D) 14

178) The legend for a map states that 1 inch on the map is equal to 20 miles in actual distance. There is a space of 2 and a half inches between two cities on the map. What figure below best represents the actual distance in kilometers between these two cities?
(1 mile = 1.61 kilometers) **(A)**
A) 31.06
B) 32.2
C) 80.5
D) 322

179) 5 boxes can be packaged in 1 and a half hours, and an extra 4 minutes per box is needed to fill out a shipping form in order to prepare the box for shipment. 14 boxes need to be packaged and prepared for shipment today. How long should it take to package all 14 boxes and prepare them for shipment? **(D)**
A) 2 hours and 52 minutes
B) 4 hours and 12 minutes
C) 5 hours and 8 minutes
D) 3 hours and 8 minutes

180) A certain brand of aquarium water treatment comes in a 2-quart size container. The treatment is repackaged into two sizes of bottles for resale. An 8-ounce size bottle of the treatment and a larger 12-ounce size bottle are sold in your store. You have 3 quarts of the treatment left in stock. You want to be able to have 25 units of the 8-ounce bottles and 20 units of the 12-ounce bottles on the shelf for sale and a further 4 quarts left in stock after you have filled all of the bottles. How many containers of the treatment do you need to buy in order to fill all of the bottles and have 4 quarts left in stock? **(A)**
A) 8
B) 14
C) 15
D) 16

181) A wastewater company measures the amount of wastewater usage per household in wastewater units ('WWU's). During one calendar quarter, the houses on a particular street had these measurements: 682, 534, 689, 783, and 985. What is the mode of wastewater usage in WWU's for this quarter for these properties? **(D)**
A) no mode
B) 451
C) 689
D) 734.6

182) Aleesha rolls a fair pair of six-sided dice. Each die has values from 1 to 6. She rolls an even number on her first roll. What is the probability that she will roll an odd number on her next roll? **(A)**

A) $1/2$
B) $1/6$
C) $2/6$
D) $6/11$

Look at the diagram below and answer questions 183 to 187

Brooke wants to put new flooring in her living room. She will buy the flooring in square pieces that measure 1 square foot each. The entire room is 8 feet by 12 feet. The bookcases are two feet deep from front to back. Flooring will not be put under the bookcases. Each piece of flooring costs $5.50. A diagram of her living room is provided.

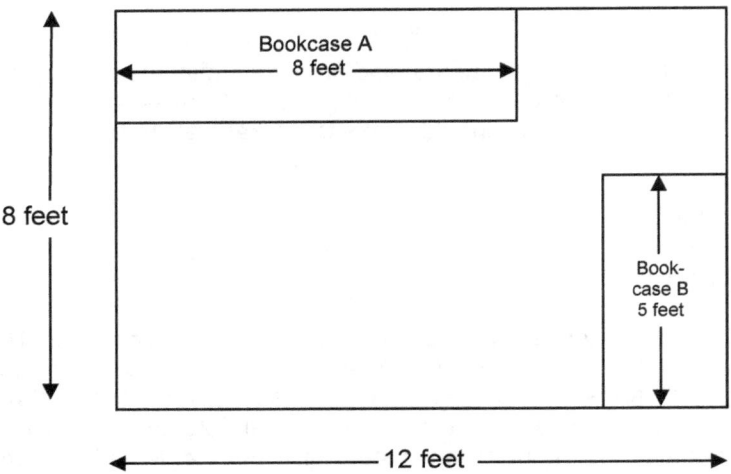

183) What is the area of the floor surface below bookcase A? **(D)**
A) 8 square feet
B) 16 square feet
C) 20 square feet
D) 64 square feet

184) What is the area of the floor surface below bookcase B? **(D)**
A) 5 square feet
B) 10 square feet
C) 14 square feet
D) 25 square feet

185) How many pieces of flooring will Brooke need to cover her floor? **(D)**
A) 120
B) 96
C) 70
D) 84

186) How much will Brooke pay to cover her living room floor? **(D)**
   A) $350
   B) $385
   C) $480
   D) $528

187) If Brooke gets a 27.5% discount off the $5.50 price per tile, about how much will she pay to cover her living room floor? **(D)**
   A) $105
   B) $255
   C) $280
   D) $382

Look at the table below and answer questions 188 to 191.

Disease or Complication	Percentage of patients with this disease that have survived and total number of patients
Cardiopulmonary and vascular	82% (602,000)
HIV/AIDS	73% (215,000)
Diabetes	89% (793,000)
Cancer and leukemia	48% (231,000)
Premature birth complications	64% (68,000)

188) Approximately how many patients with diabetes have survived? **(M)**
   A) 58,050
   B) 87,230
   C) 156,950
   D) 705,770

189) The highest number of deaths occurred as a result of which disease? **(D)**
   A) Cardiovascular an pulmonary disease
   B) HIV/AIDS
   C) Cancer and leukemia
   D) Premature birth complications

190) Approximately how many cancer and leukemia patients have not survived? **(D)**
   A) 24,500
   B) 110,900
   C) 120,000
   D) 231,000

191) The total number of deaths from the two least fatal diseases amounted to which figure below? **(D)**
   A) 82,530
   B) 208,960
   C) 1,186,040
   D) 1,199,410

192) Which one of the following is a solution to the following ordered pairs of equations? **(A)**
−3x − 1 = y
x + 7 = y
A) (5, −2)
B) (−2, 5)
C) (2, 5)
D) (5, 2)

193) Which of the following shows the numbers ordered from greatest to least? **(M)**
A) −1/3 , 1/7 , 1 , 1/5
B) −1/3 , 1/5 , 1/7 , 1
C) −1/3 , 1 , 1/7 , 1/5
D) 1 , 1/5 , 1/7 , −1/3

194) If 3x − 9 = −18, then x = ? **(D)**
A) −6
B) 6
C) −3
D) 3

195) Evaluate: $2x^2 + 8x$ if x = 7 **(D)**
A) 154
B) 105
C) 98
D) 56

196) If $f_1(x) = x^2 + x$, what is the value of $f_1(5)$? **(A)**
A) 5
B) 10
C) 25
D) 30

197) $4^{11} \times 4^8$ = ? **(D)**
A) 16^{19}
B) 4^{19}
C) 8^{19}
D) 4^{88}

198) Expand the polynomial: (x − 5)(3x + 8) **(D)**
A) $3x^2 − 7x − 40$
B) $3x^2 − 7x + 40$
C) $3x^2 + 23x − 40$
D) $3x^2 + 23x + 40$

199) If $\sqrt{9z + 18} = 9$, then z = ? **(A)**

A) −1   B) 6   C) 7   D) 63

200) If $z = \dfrac{x}{1-y}$, then y = ? **(A)**

A) $\dfrac{z}{x}$ B) $\dfrac{x}{z} - 1$ C) $-\dfrac{x}{z} + 1$ D) $z - zx$

TABE 9 & 10 Practice Test 2

201) An art and craft store received $7,375 for sales of a certain type of scrapbook this year. If these scrapbooks were sold for $59 each, how many of them were sold this year? **(E)**
A) 135
B) 125
C) 120
D) 75

202) The increases and decreases this week for the sales of five products in units were as follows: 52, −14, 37, −28, 61? What was the total increase or decrease in units for these products for the week? **(E)**
A) −108
B) 60
C) 78
D) 108

203) $6/25$ of the inventory has been sold this month. Approximately what percentage of the inventory has been sold? **(E)**
A) 0.24%
B) 2.40%
C) 24.0%
D) 4.167%

204) Changes to monthly cash flow is reported as a decimal figure, which is calculated by dividing the net change in cash flow into the previous month's cash flow. Last month, the change to cash flow was 0.40. What percentage best represents the change to cash flow for last month? **(E)**
A) 0.40%
B) 4.00%
C) 40.0%
D) 400%

205) The temperature on Saturday was 62°F at 5:00 PM and 38°F at 11:00 PM. If the temperature fell at a constant rate on Saturday, what was the temperature at 9:00 PM? **(M)**
A) 58°F
B) 54°F
C) 50°F
D) 46°F

206) Hot dogs sell for $2.50 each, and hamburgers sell for $4 each. A family went out to eat and bought 3 hamburgers. They also bought hot dogs. The total cost of their food was $22. How many hot dogs did they buy? **(M)**
A) 2
B) 3
C) 4
D) 5

207) A painter needs to paint 8 rooms, each of which has a surface area of 2000 square feet. If one bucket of paint covers 900 square feet, what is the fewest number of buckets of paint that must be purchased to complete all 8 rooms? **(M)**
A) 3
B) 17
C) 18
D) 19

208) Soon Li jogged 3.6 miles in ¾ of an hour. What was her average jogging speed in miles per hour? **(M)**
A) 4.8
B) 4.6
C) 4.2
D) 2.7

209) The price of a certain book is reduced from $60 to $45 at the end of the semester. By what percent is the price of the book reduced? **(M)**
A) 15%
B) 20%
C) 25%
D) 33%

210) The ratio of males to females in the senior year class of Carson Heights High School was 6 to 7. If the total number of students in the class was 117, how many males were in the class? **(M)**
A) 48
B) 54
C) 56
D) 58

211) Members of a weight loss group report their individual weight loss to their group leader every week. During the week, the following amounts in pounds were reported: 1, 1, 3, 2, 4, 3, 1, 2, and 1. What is the mean of the weight loss for the group? **(D)**
A) 1 pound
B) 2 pounds
C) 3 pounds
D) 4 pounds

212) A family has 5 children. The ages of 5 siblings are: 2, 5, 7, 12, and x. If the mean age of the 5 siblings is 8 years old, what is the age (x) of the 5th sibling? **(A)**
A) 8
B) 10
C) 12
D) 14

213) Work-motion scores for one employee for each day of the week were as follows: 8.19, 7.59, 8.25, 7.35, and 9.10. What is the median of this employee's scores? **(D)**
A) 7.59
B) 8.19
C) 8.25
D) 8.096

214) The table below shows the relationship between the total number of chicken sandwiches a customer can buy and the total price for each order. If a customer takes the deal that has the lowest price per sandwich, what will the customer pay per sandwich? **(M)**
2 chicken sandwiches for $17.50
4 chicken sandwiches for $34.40
8 chicken sandwiches for $68.00
A) $4.00
B) $8.00
C) $8.50
D) $9.50

215) A pizzeria sold 15 cheese pizzas, 10 pepperoni pizzas, and 5 vegetable pizzas one day. Cheese pizzas sell for $10 each; pepperoni pizzas sell for $12, and the total sales of all three types of pizza for that day was $310. What price is charged for 1 vegetable pizza? **(D)**
A) $5
B) $8
C) $9
D) $10

216) Shanika works as a car salesperson. She earns $1,000 a month in basic pay, plus $390 for each car she sells. If she wants to earn at least $4,000 this month, what is the minimum number of cars that she must sell this month? **(M)**
A) 6
B) 7
C) 8
D) 9

217) One private airplane flew at a constant speed, traveling 780 miles in 2 hours. How many miles did this plane travel in the last 40 minutes of its journey? **(M)**
A) 120
B) 180
C) 200
D) 260

218) A horse ran 12 furlongs in 2 minutes and 48 seconds. Assuming that the same amount of time was spent on each furlong, how many seconds does it take the horse to run one furlong? **(D)**
A) 0.014 seconds
B) 0.14 seconds
C) 1.40 seconds
D) 14 seconds

219) A national report states that 30 out of every 100 television viewers watch TV for more than 25 hours her week. If there are 3,200 television viewers in Newtown, how many television viewers in Newtown watch TV for more than 25 hours per week? **(D)**
A) 320
B) 750
C) 960
D) 1,067

220) An item costs $22 each if the customer collects it in person from the store, and an extra $3 for postage and handling is charged per item if the customer wants the item sent by courier. This week, 32 customers purchased this item and requested that the item be sent by courier. How much money in total did the store make on the items sold to these 32 customers? **(M)**
A) $800
B) $704
C) $575
D) $96

221) $107\frac{3}{8}$ yards of adhesive plastic is needed to complete one work order and $96\frac{1}{8}$ yards of adhesive plastic is needed for another work order. How many yards of adhesive plastic is needed in total in order to complete both of these work orders? **(M)**
A) $193\frac{1}{8}$
B) $203\frac{1}{2}$
C) $193\frac{1}{4}$
D) $203\frac{1}{4}$

222) A vat contains 163.75 units of red colorant, 107.50 units of blue colorant, 91.25 units of yellow colorant, and 10.30 units of black colorant. Which of the following represents, in terms of units, how full the vat is after these 4 colorants have been placed in it? **(E)**
   A) 362.50
   B) 371.50
   C) 372.80
   D) 373.50

223) A customer who owns a small hotel has ordered 10 new quilts. Each quilt requires 2 yards of red fabric for the front, 1 yard of blue fabric for the front, and a further 3 yards of blue fabric for the back. The quilts need to have an embellishment in gold, and a total amount of 6 yards of gold fabric is needed to make the embellishments for all 5 quilts. Each quilt also has edging in white, and half a yard of white material is needed for the edging for each quilt. How many yards of fabric in total will be needed to complete this order? **(D)**
   A) 7.7
   B) 77
   C) 3.85
   D) 38.5

224) Fence panels are going to be placed along one side of a field. Each panel is 8 feet 6 inches long. 11 panels are needed to cover the entire side of the field. How long is the field? **(D)**
   A) 60 feet 6 inches
   B) 72 feet 8 inches
   C) 93 feet 6 inches
   D) 102 feet 8 inches

225) The area of a square floor is 64 square units. The floor needs to be covered entirely with tiles. Each floor tile is 4 square units. How many tiles are needed to cover the floor? **(D)**
   A) 8
   B) 12
   C) 16
   D) 24

226) The base of a cylinder is at a right angle to its sides. The radius of the base of the cylinder measures 5 centimeters. The height of the cylinder is 10 centimeters. What is the volume of this container in cubic centimeters? **(A)**
   A) 785
   B) 157
   C) 78.5
   D) 31.4

227) Cone A has a base radius of 9 and a height of 18. Cone B has a base radius of 3 and a height of 6. Which number below expresses the ratio of the volume of Cone A to Cone B? **(A)**
   A) 27
   B) $1/27$
   C) 3
   D) $1/6$

228) 500 units of a particular item can be purchased for 72 cents each from one supplier or from a different supplier for $350 for all 500 units. Sales tax of 5.5% is to be added to either purchase. What is the best total price for the items, including tax? **(M)**
   A) $350.00
   B) $360.00
   C) $369.25
   D) $379.80

229) Seven members of a support group are trying to gain weight. So far, the weight gain in kilograms for each of the seven members of the group is: 12, 15, 3, 7, 21, 14, and 12. What is the range of the amount of weight gain for this support group? **(D)**
A) 18
B) 12
C) 14
D) 7

230) Looking at our seven group members from the question above, what is the mode? **(D)**
A) 18
B) 12
C) 14
D) 7

Look at the graph below and answer questions 231 to 234.

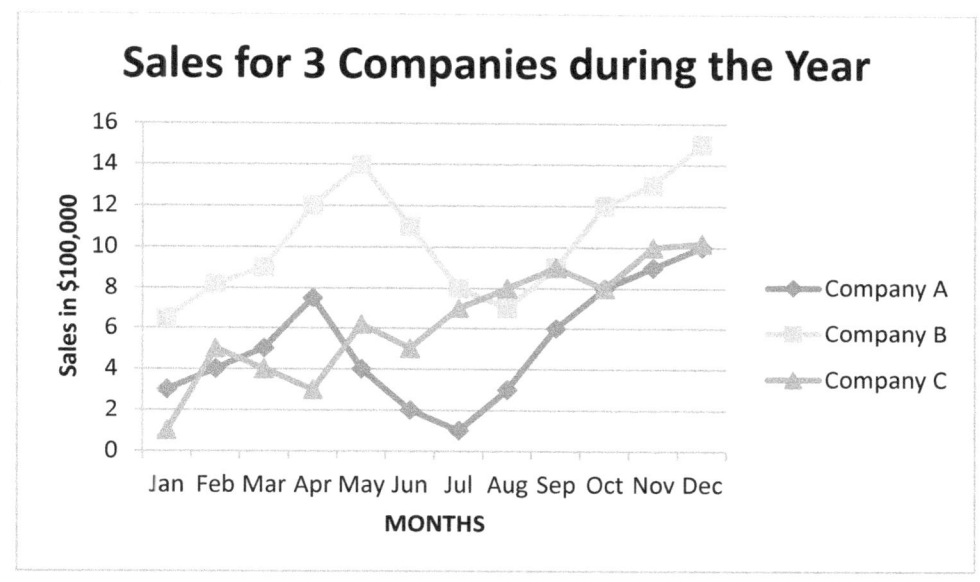

231) Which company had the highest sales figure for July? **(M)**
A) Company A
B) Company B
C) Company C
D) Companies B and C

232) What was the approximate sales figure for Company A for April? **(M)**
A) $300,000
B) $500,000
C) $790,000
D) $1,200,000

233) What was the approximate difference in sales for Company B and Company C in May? **(M)**
A) Company B's sales were $800,000 more than Company C's.
B) Company C's sales were $800,000 more than Company B's.
C) Company B's sales were $80,000 less than Company C's.
D) Company C's sales were $80,000 less than Company B's.

234) The combined total of sales for all three of the companies was greatest during which month of the year? **(M)**
   A) December
   B) November
   C) May
   D) April

Look at the bar chart below and answer questions 235 to 238.

The chart below shows data on the number of vehicles involved in accidents in Cedar Valley.

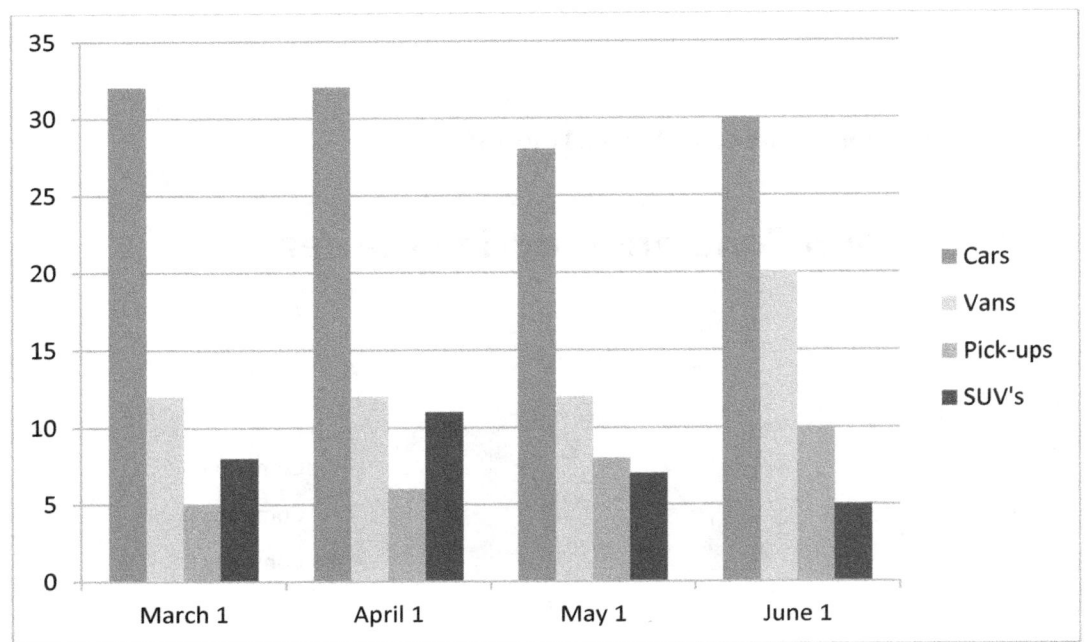

235) Which vehicle had the smallest number of accidents for May 1 and June 1 combined? **(M)**
   A) Cars
   B) Vans
   C) Pick-ups
   D) SUV's

236) Which vehicle accounted for the largest number of accidents all four dates in total? **(M)**
   A) Cars
   B) Vans
   C) Pick-ups
   D) SUV's

237) About how many vans and SUV's were involved in accidents in Cedar Valley on March 1? **(M)**
   A) 15
   B) 17
   C) 20
   D) 37

238) About how many accidents involved pick-ups for May 1 and June 1 in total? **(M)**
   A) 10
   B) 11
   C) 12
   D) 17

Look at the pie chart below and answer questions 239 to 241.

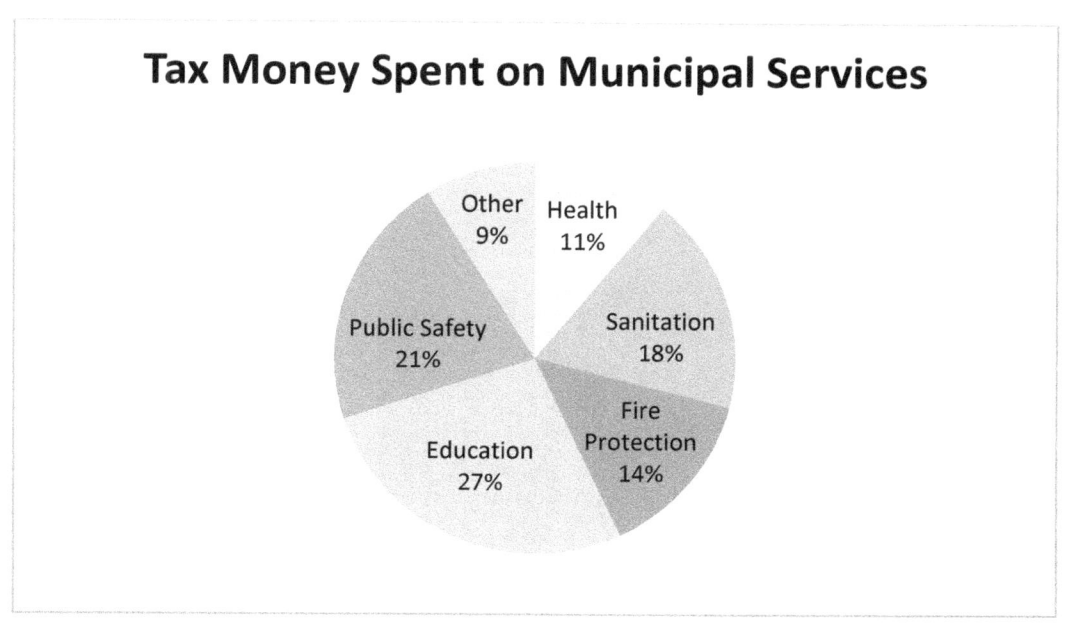

239) According to the chart, the two highest categories accounted for what percentage of use in total? **(M)**
A) 32%
B) 41%
C) 48%
D) 52%

240) If $5,275,300 in total tax money was spend on all municipal services, how much was spend on education? **(M)**
A) $474,777
B) $580,283
C) $1,107,813
D) $1,424,331

241) For next year, $6,537,200 in total tax money is budgeted for all municipal services. Each category is allocated the same percentage of next year's budget as the actual percentage spent for the current year. What is the budget amount for public safety? **(M)**
A) $915,208
B) $1,107,813
C) $1,372,812
D) $1,765,004

242) Which of the following points lies on the graph of $10x + 3y = 29$? **(D)**
A) (3, 2)
B) (2, 3)
C) (1, 6)
D) (6, 1)

243) If $f_2(x) = \sqrt{x} + 3$ and $f_1(x) = 3x + 1$, what is the value of $f_1(f_2(9))$? **(A)**
  A) $\sqrt{28} + 3$
  B) 19
  C) 28
  D) 6

244) Perform the operation: $\sqrt{6} \cdot (\sqrt{40} + \sqrt{6})$ **(A)**
  A) $\sqrt{240} + \sqrt{6}$
  B) $\sqrt{46} + 6$
  C) 46
  D) $4\sqrt{15} + 6$

245) $(x - 9y)^2 = ?$ **(D)**
  A) $x^2 + 81y^2$
  B) $x^2 - 18xy - 18y^2$
  C) $x^2 - 18xy + 81y^2$
  D) $x^2 + 18xy - 81y^2$

246) $6 + \dfrac{x}{4} \geq 22$, then $x \geq$? **(D)**
  A) −8
  B) 64
  C) −64
  D) 128

247) $(x^2 - x - 12) \div (x - 4) = ?$ **(D)**
  A) $(x + 3)$
  B) $(x - 3)$
  C) $(-x + 3)$
  D) $(-x - 3)$

248) Which of the following expressions is equivalent to: $18xy - 24x^2y - 48y^2x^2$? **(D)**
  A) $6xy(3 - 4x - 8xy)$
  B) $3xy(6 - 8x - 16xy)$
  C) $6x^2y(3 - 4 - 8y)$
  D) $6xy(3 - 4x + 8xy)$

249) $\sqrt{15x^3} \times \sqrt{8x^2}$ **(D)**
  A) $\sqrt{23x^5}$
  B) $2x^2\sqrt{30x^3}$
  C) $2x^2\sqrt{30x}$
  D) $\sqrt{23x^6}$

250) What is the value of the expression $2x^2 + 5xy - y^2$ when $x = 4$ and $y = -3$? **(D)**
  A) −37
  B) −19
  C) 86
  D) 101

TABE 9 & 10 Practice Test 3

251) A store sells domestic cleaning products. A certain type of liquid cleaner is sold in increments of 1/4 of a cup. Each 1/4 of a cup costs 50 cents. One customer buys $10\frac{1}{4}$ cups of this cleaner. How much will she pay for this purchase? **(M)**
A) $5.13
B) $5.50
C) $10.50
D) $20.50

252) The cost of sales figures each month for a company's first five months of business this year were: $723, $618, $576, $812, and $984. What was the total cost of sales for the first five months of business this year? **(E)**
A) $743
B) $3,623
C) $3,713
D) $3,722

253) 4 out of every 5 employee-satisfaction questionnaires have been completed and returned. If a company has 250 total employees, and every employee must complete and return the questionnaire, how many questionnaires have not been completed and returned? **(E)**
A) 4
B) 5
C) 50
D) 200

254) A flower store sells poinsettia plants for $20 during December and for $12 during January. In December, 55 customers purchased poinsettias, and 20 customers purchased them in January. How much money did the store receive for poinsettia sales during December and January? **(M)**
A) $240
B) $1,060
C) $1,100
D) $1,340

255) During each flight, a flight attendant is required to count the number of passengers on board the aircraft. The morning flight had 52 passengers more than the evening flight, and there were 540 passengers in total on the two flights that day. How many passengers were there on the evening flight? **(M)**
A) 244
B) 296
C) 488
D) 540

256) A cafeteria serves spaghetti to senior citizens on Fridays. The spaghetti comes prepared in large containers, and each container holds 15 servings of spaghetti. The cafeteria is expecting 82 senior citizens this Friday. What is the least number of containers of spaghetti that the cafeteria will need in order to serve all 82 people? **(M)**
A) 4
B) 5
C) 6
D) 7

257) A caterpillar travels 10.5 inches in 45 seconds. How far will it travel in 6 minutes? **(M)**
A) 45 inches
B) 63 inches
C) 64 inches
D) 84 inches

258) Each week, a company tabulates the results of customer satisfaction surveys by region and calculates the bonuses to be paid. The company has four regions, each of which has one salesperson. Salespeople in each region receive bonuses based on the amount of positive customer feedback they receive. The results of the surveys were as follows:
Region 1: 40 positive customer feedback results
Region 2: 30 positive customer feedback results
Region 3: 20 positive customer feedback results
Region 4: 30 positive customer feedback results
If the four salespeople received $540 in bonuses in total, how much bonus money does the company pay each individual salesperson per satisfied customer? **(D)**
A) $4.00
B) $4.50
C) $4.90
D) $5.00

259) Return on investment (ROI) percentages for seven companies were: –2%, 5%, 7.5%, 14%, 17%, 1.3%, –3%. Which figure below best approximates the mean ROI for the seven companies? **(D)**
A) 2%
B) 5.7%
C) 6.25%
D) 7.5%

260) A plumber charges $100 per job, plus $25 per hour worked. He is going to do 5 jobs this month. He will earn a total of $4,000. How many hours will he work this month? **(M)**
A) 10
B) 40
C) 80
D) 140

261) The number of visitors a museum had on Tuesday (T) was twice as much as the number of visitors it had on Monday (M). The number of visitors it had on Wednesday (W) was 20% greater than that on Tuesday. Which equation can be used to calculate the total number of visitors to the museum for the three days? **(M)**
A) 5.4M
B) 2M + T + W
C) M + 1.2T + W
D) W + .20W + 2T + M

262) The students at Lyndon High School have been asked about their plans to attend the Homecoming Dance. The chart below shows the responses of each grade level by percentages. Which figure below best approximates the percentage of the total number of students from all four grades who will attend the dance? Note that each grade level has roughly the same number of students. **(M)**

	Will Attend	Will Not Attend	Undecided
Freshmen:	45%	24%	31%
Sophomores:	30%	45%	25%
Juniors:	38%	20%	42%
Seniors:	30%	25%	45%

A) 25%
B) 35%
C) 45%
D) 55%

263) An employment agency for temporary employees charges clients $15 per hour for each hour the temporary employee works. The agency pays each temporary employee $12 an hour and retains the difference as a commission. The agency had 10 employees who worked 40 hours each this week. How much did the agency make on commission for these 10 employees this week? **(M)**
A) $30.00
B) $120.00
C) $1,200.00
D) $4,800.00

264) 49 out of the 50 items in a company's product line had above average sales this month. What percentage of the items in the product line had above average sales this month? **(E)**
A) 0.098%
B) 0.98%
C) 9.80%
D) 98%

265) Sales each day for the past five days have been as follows: $90, $85, $85, $105, $110. What was the daily average sales amount during this five-day period? **(M)**
A) $25
B) $85
C) $90
D) $95

266) A fabric store sells ribbon in 3-inch or one-foot increments. One customer wanted two types of ribbon, and she bought $8^{3}/_{4}$ feet of one type of ribbon and $7^{1}/_{2}$ feet of another type. How much ribbon did this customer buy in total? **(M)**
A) 7 feet and 6 inches
B) 8 feet and 9 inches
C) 15 feet and 3 inches
D) 16 feet and 3 inches

267) Hours spent on a work order are recorded by the tenth of an hour in 6 minute increments. For a particular work order, $28^{3}/_{10}$ hours in total have been budgeted. $7^{9}/_{10}$ hours have already been spent on the work order. Which amount below represents the amount of time left for this work order? **(M)**
A) $36^{1}/_{5}$
B) $35^{6}/_{10}$
C) $20^{2}/_{5}$
D) $20^{3}/_{5}$

268) A decorative stone mix requires 2 parts of white gravel for every 3 parts of blue slate chippings. An order requires 147 parts of blue slate chippings. How many parts of white gravel should be added? **(D)**
A) 73.5
B) 88.0
C) 98.0
D) 220.5

269) A factory manufactures absorbent disposable products that consist of a single layer of absorbent cotton wadding on the inside and a double layer polyvinyl carbonate sheeting on the outside. Each layer of absorbent cotton wadding is 18 inches long, and each layer of polyvinyl carbonate sheeting is 19 inches long. 18 of these products need to be made for a single order. How many feet of materials in total will be required to manufacture this order? **(M)**
A) 55.5
B) 56
C) 84
D) 666

270) An automotive store can buy a case containing 24 bottles of motor oil for $50 a case wholesale. Individual bottles of this brand of motor oil cost $2.50 per bottle wholesale. What is the best price the store will pay if it buys 100 bottles of motor oil wholesale? **(M)**
A) $200.00
B) $200.10
C) $202.50
D) $210.00

271) Flavored rice cakes sold in the United States are measured in ounces, and units sold overseas are measured in grams. 39 ounces of flavoring are needed for a batch of rice cakes for the United States and 1,190.7 grams of the same flavoring are needed for another batch of rice cakes to be sold overseas. How much flavoring is needed for both batches in total?
(1 ounce = 28.350 grams) **(D)**
A) 81 ounces
B) 40.48 ounces
C) 43.38 grams
D) 2,297.35 grams

272) A ceiling is 25 feet wide and 35 feet long. The ceiling is to be covered with square ceiling tiles that measure 6 inches by 6 inches each. How many of these square ceiling tiles are needed to install this ceiling? **(D)**
A) 1,750
B) 3,500
C) 480
D) 875

273) This month, a nurse dispensed 1,275,000 milligrams of medication to patients. How many grams of medication were dispensed? **(M)**
A) 127.5
B) 1,275
C) 12,750
D) 127,500,000

274) A basketball has a diameter of 10 inches. Which figure below best represents the volumetric capacity of the basketball in cubic centimeters? (1 inch = 2.54 centimeters) **(A)**
A) 32
B) 523
C) 4,824
D) 8,576

275) Cell phone covers are sold for a retail price of $12 per unit. This amounts to a 525% markup over the cost for each unit. How much does each unit cost? **(M)**
A) $0.192
B) $1.92
C) $6.25
D) $0.75

276) The perimeter of a rectangle is 350 feet and the width of the shortest side is 75 feet. What is the measurement of the length of the rectangle? **(D)**
   A) 10 feet
   B) 90 feet
   C) 95 feet
   D) 100 feet

277) Storage boxes for rice flour measure 3 feet by 3 feet by 2 feet each. The first box is ⅙ full, the second box is ½ full, and the third box is ⅔ full. A factory wants to replenish its supply of rice flour so that it will have three full boxes. The rice flour costs 9 cents a cubic inch. To the nearest dollar, what will it cost to replenish the stock in the three boxes? (1 cubic foot = 1,728 cubic inches) **(D)**
   A) $270
   B) $466
   C) $998
   D) $4,666

278) A entertainer pulls colored ribbons out of a box at random for a dance routine. The box contains 5 red ribbons and 6 blue ribbons. The other ribbons in the box are green. If a ribbon is pulled out of the box at random, the probability that the ribbon is red is ⅓. How many green ribbons are in the box? **(A)**
   A) 3
   B) 4
   C) 5
   D) 6

279) Find the median of the following: 2.5, 9.4, 3.1, 1.7, 3.2, 8.2, 4.5, 6.4, 7.8 **(D)**
   A) 3.2
   B) 4.5
   C) 5.2
   D) 6.4

Look at the diagram and information below and answer questions 280 to 282.

Each square in the diagram below is one yard wide and one yard long. The gray area of the diagram represents New Town's water reservoir. The white area represents the surrounding conservation park.

280) What is the perimeter in yards of the reservoir? **(D)**
   A) 18
   B) 28
   C) 32
   D) 63

281) What is the area in square yards of the surrounding conservation park? **(A)**
   A) 18
   B) 44
   C) 45
   D) 46

282) Which of the following ratios represents the area of the reservoir to the area of the surrounding conservation park? **(A)**
   A) 2:5
   B) 9:23
   C) 17:32
   D) 18:44

Look at the diagram below and answer questions 283 to 285.

A packaging company secures their packages with plastic strapping prior to shipment. The box is 20 inches in height, 22 inches in depth, and twenty 42 inches in length. For certain packages, 15 extra inches of strapping is used to make a handle on the top of the package to carry it. The strapping is wrapped around the length and width of the entire package, as shown in the following diagram:

283) How many inches of strapping is needed for one package, including making the handle? **(D)**
   A) 124
   B) 128
   C) 252
   D) 267

284) How many inches of strapping is needed to wrap 25 packages if no handles are used? **(D)**
   A) 3,100
   B) 3,200
   C) 6,300
   D) 6,675

285) The volume of the box must be declared prior to shipment. What is the volume in cubic inches of the box shown above? **(A)**
   A) 8,800
   B) 16,800
   C) 18,480
   D) 20,328

Look at the information below and answer questions 286 to 288.

Chantelle took a test that had four parts. The total number of questions on each part is given in the table below, as is the number of questions that Chantelle answered correctly.

Part	Total Number of Questions	Number of Questions Answered Correctly
1	15	12
2	25	20
3	35	32
4	45	32

286) How many points in total were there on parts 3 and 4 of the test? **(M)**
   A) 60
   B) 64
   C) 70
   D) 80

287) Which fraction below best represents the relationship of Chantelle's incorrect answers on Part 1 to the total points on Part 1? **(M)**
   A) 1/5
   B) 1/3
   C) 4/5
   D) 4/6

288) What was Chantelle's percentage score of correct answers for the entire test? **(M)**
   A) 75%
   B) 80%
   C) 86%
   D) 90%

289) What number is next in this sequence? 2, 4, 8, 16 **(M)**
   A) 18
   B) 20
   C) 24
   D) 32

290) Find the x and y intercepts of the following equation: $5x^2 + 4y^2 = 120$ **(D)**
   A) $(0, \sqrt{30})$ and $(\sqrt{24}, 0)$
   B) $(0, 30)$ and $(24, 0)$
   C) $(\sqrt{24}, 0)$ and $(0, \sqrt{30})$
   D) $(30, 0)$ and $(0, 24)$

291) Consider a two-dimensional linear graph where x = 4 and y = 15. The line crosses the y axis at 3. What is the slope of this line? **(A)**

A) $\frac{1}{15}$

B) 3

C) $-\frac{1}{3}$

D) −3

292) Evaluate: $x^2 - 5x - 9$ if x = 8 **(D)**
A) 5
B) 15
C) 40
D) 64

293) Solve for x: 5x − 9 = 6 **(M)**
A) 3
B) 6
C) 8
D) 9

294) Which of the following steps will solve the equation for x: 18 = 3(x + 5) **(D)**
A) Subtract 5 from each side of the equation, and then divide both sides by 3.
B) Subtract 18 from each side of the equation, and then divide both sides by 5.
C) Multiply both x and 5 by 3 on the right side of the equation. Then subtract 15 from each side of the equation.
D) Divide each side of the equation by 3. Then subtract 5 from both sides of the equation.

295) Express 81 as a logarithmic function. **(A)**
A) $81 = \log_2 9$
B) $2 = \log_9 81$
C) $9 = \log_2 81$
D) $81 = \log_9 2$

296) $\sqrt{5} \times \sqrt{3} = ?$ **(D)**
A) 15
B) $\sqrt{8}$
C) $\sqrt{15}$
D) $5\sqrt{3}$

297) Which of the following expressions is equivalent to $\frac{x}{5} + \frac{y}{2}$? **(A)**

A) $\frac{x+y}{7}$

B) $\frac{2x+5y}{10}$

C) $\frac{5x+2y}{10}$

D) $\frac{2x+5y}{7}$

298) Which of the following values of x is a possible solution to the inequality?: $-3x + 14 < 5$ **(M)**
   A) −3.1
   B) 2.80
   C) 2.25
   D) 3.15

299) $(x − 2y)(2x^2 − y) = ?$ **(D)**
   A) $2x^3 − 4x^2y + 2y^2 − xy$
   B) $2x^3 + 2y^2 − 5xy$
   C) $2x^3 − 4x^2y + 2y^2 + xy$
   D) $2x^3 + 4x^2y + 2y^2 − xy$

300) $20 − \frac{3x}{4} \geq 17$, then $x \leq ?$ **(M)**
   A) −12
   B) −4
   C) −3
   D) 4

TABE 9 & 10 Practice Test 4

301) Moisture changes inside a particular structure over 4 weeks were as follows. Week 1: –14 milligrams; Week 2: 15 milligrams; Week 3: –12 milligrams: Week 4: –5 milligrams. What figure below represents the change in the moisture content of this structure from week 3 to week 4? **(E)**
A) –17
B) –7
C) 7
D) –16

302) A salesperson gets $1,250 basic pay per month plus a $12 commission every time a customer orders more than $100 worth of products. This month, the salesperson had 32 customers who ordered more than $100 worth of products. How much did the salesperson earn in total this month? **(E)**
A) $866
B) $1262
C) $1634
D) $1643

303) A farm store received $310 for sales insecticide. If this insecticide is sold for $12.40 each, how many of them did the store sell this month? **(E)**
A) 6
B) 25
C) 38
D) 52

304) The ratio of bags of apples to bags of oranges in a store is 2 to 3. If there are 44 bags of apples in the store, how many bags of oranges are there? **(M)**
A) 33
B) 48
C) 55
D) 66

305) A dance academy had 300 students at the beginning of January. It lost 5% of its students during the month. However, 15 new students joined the academy on the last day of the month. If this pattern continues for the next two months, how many students will there be at the academy at the end of March? **(M)**
A) 285
B) 300
C) 310
D) 315

306) The price of a wool coat is reduced 12.5% at the end of the winter. If the original price of the coat was $120, what will the price be after the reduction? **(E)**
A) $108.00
B) $107.50
C) $105.70
D) $105.00

307) A factory produces 20 times as many functioning microchips than defective chips. If the factory produced 11,235 chips in total last week, how many of them were defective? **(M)**
A) 535
B) 561
C) 1,070
D) 10,700

308) A town has recently suffered a flood. The total cost, represented by variable C, which is available to accommodate R number of residents in emergency housing is represented by the equation C = $750R + $2,550. If the town has a total of $55,000 available for emergency housing, what is the greatest number of residents that it can house? **(D)**
A) 68
B) 69
C) 70
D) 71

309) The data on kilowatt-hours of usage per day for one electricity user was as follows: 2.5, 9.4, 3.1, 1.7, 3.2, 8.2, 4.5, 6.4, 7.8. What was the median value of kilowatt usage for this customer? **(D)**
A) 3.2
B) 4.5
C) 5.2
D) 6.4

310) An employee was able to produce the following number of units each hour that he worked: 89, 65, 75, 68, 82, 74, and 86. What is the mean of the number of units that he produced per hour? **(D)**
A) 24
B) 74
C) 75
D) 77

311) There are 8 cars in a parking lot. 7 of the cars are 2, 3, 4, 5, 9, 10, and 12 years old, respectively. If the average age of the 8 cars is 6 years old, how old is the 8th car? **(A)**
A) 3 years old
B) 4 years old
C) 6 years old
D) 8 years old

312) The fine for speeding violations is $50 per violation. The fine for other violations is $20 per violation. This week, there were 60 speeding violations, 30 parking violations, and 90 other violations. The total collected for all three types of violations was $6,000. What is the fine for each parking violation? **(A)**
A) $20
B) $30
C) $40
D) $100

313) The price of a sofa at a furniture store was x dollars on Wednesday this week. On Thursday, the price of the sofa was reduced by 10% of Wednesday's price. On Friday, the price of the sofa was reduced again by 15% of Thursday's price. Which of the following expressions can be used to calculate the price of the sofa on Friday? **(A)**
A) $(0.75)x$
B) $(0.90)(0.85)x$
C) $(0.10)(0.15)x$
D) $(0.10)(0.85)x$

314) A clothing store sells jackets and jeans at a discount during a sales period. T represents the number of jackets sold and N represents the number of jeans sold. The total amount of money the store collected for sales of jeans and jackets during the sales period was $4,000. The amount of money earned from selling jackets was one-third of that earned from selling jeans. The jeans sold for $20 a pair. How many pairs of jeans did the store sell during the sales period? **(A)**
A) 15
B) 20
C) 150
D) 200

315) Statistics indicate that 81% of the residents of Springfield are satisfied with the services they receive from city hall. What decimal number represents this percentage? **(E)**
A) 0.00081
B) 0.00810
C) 0.08100
D) 0.81000

316) An accountant had two projects to complete for one particular client this month. She spent $37^{2}/_{5}$ hours on the first project and $25^{4}/_{5}$ hours on the other project. How many hours did she spend on projects for this client this month? **(M)**
A) $63^{1}/_{5}$
B) $62^{1}/_{5}$
C) $53^{1}/_{5}$
D) $52^{1}/_{5}$

317) Research indicates that the best customer to sales-clerk ratio for high-end luxury stores is 3 to 1. A particular store is expecting 15 customers tomorrow. How many sales clerks should it have available? **(M)**
A) 1
B) 3
C) 5
D) 12

318) It took from 9:15 AM to 10:25 AM for a painter to paint 7 square yards. The painter has to paint 17.5 square yards in total for this particular job. If he continues working at the same pace, what time will he finish painting? **(D)**
A) 11:10 AM
B) 11:10 PM
C) 11:30 AM
D) 12:10 PM

319) 1235.35 units of product A, 567.55 units of product B, and 347.25 units of product C are needed for the order that is currently being processed. Which of the following represents the total number of units for all of the products in this order? **(E)**
A) 2150.15
B) 2149.15
C) 1802.90
D) 1582.60

320) Soft drink is purchased for resale in 20 gallon containers. A store has one container with $19^{3}/_{4}$ gallons and another with $14^{3}/_{4}$ gallons of soft drink. How much soft drink does the store have in total in these two containers? **(M)**
A) 5
B) $33^{1}/_{2}$
C) $33^{3}/_{4}$
D) $34^{1}/_{2}$

321) A company that manufactures aluminum products started the month with $102^{7}/_{18}$ yards of aluminum sheeting. $24^{11}/_{18}$ yards of aluminum sheeting was left at the end of the month. Which figure below represents the amount of aluminum sheeting used this month in yards? **(M)**
A) $77^{7}/_{9}$
B) $78^{7}/_{9}$
C) $77^{2}/_{9}$
D) $78^{2}/_{9}$

322) A medical professional works in a hospital unit that has 14 patients. It takes him $1^{3}/_{4}$ hours in total to prepare medications and treatments when he arrives at work every morning. He spends 15 minutes doing files and administrative work for each patient on his unit per day. He works an 8-hour daily shift. How much time does he have left to devote to other tasks each day after he has prepared medications and treatments and finished his files and administrative work? **(M)**
A) 2 hours and 5 minutes
B) 2 hours and 15 minutes
C) 2 hours and 45 minutes
D) 3 hours and 30 minutes

323) Six members of staff have received the following scores on their annual performance reviews: 96, 89, 63, 98, 81, 77. What was the average annual performance review score for these 6 employees? **(M)**
A) 73.5
B) 79.5
C) 82.5
D) 84.0

324) The radius of circle A is 5 centimeters. The radius of circle B is 3 centimeters. Which of the following statements is true? **(A)**
A) The difference between the areas of the circles is approximately 6.28.
B) The difference between the areas of the circles is approximately 28.26.
C) The difference between the circumferences of the circles is approximately 6.28.
D) The difference between the circumferences of the circles is approximately 12.56.

325) A large tire has a radius of 10 inches. A smaller tire has a radius of 6 inches. If the large tire is going to travel 360 revolutions, approximately how many more revolutions does the small tire need to make to cover the same distance? **(A)**
A) 120
B) 240
C) 360
D) 600

326) A rectangle has a length of 18 inches and a width of 10 inches. What is the perimeter of the rectangle in inches? **(D)**
A) 36
B) 46
C) 56
D) 180

327) The circumference of the floor space of a circular arena is approximately 1,017.36 feet. A partition needs to be placed in the middle of the floor space in order to create two equal semi-circular parts. What is the measurement in yards of the partition? **(A)**
A) 6
B) 18
C) 108
D) 180

328) Product A normally costs $20 per unit. With a membership card, a $4 discount per unit is given. The store has started to offer the same percentage discount on Product B. Product B normally costs $16 per unit. What figure below represents the purchase cost of Product B after the discount? **(M)**
A) $3.20
B) $4.00
C) $12.00
D) $12.80

329) A rectangular-shaped container has a side length of 10 inches, a height of 7 inches, and a width of 5 inches. Which figure below best approximates the volume of the container in gallons? (1 gallon = 231 cubic inches) **(A)**
A) 1.52
B) 152
C) 350
D) 80,850

330) A herbal therapy product comes as a liquid that needs to be diluted with organic wheat grass juice. To get the correct concentration, 3 ounces of herbal therapy product has to be added to every 2 cups of organic wheat grass juice that is used. A mixture that contains 14 cups of organic wheat grass juice needs to be made. How many ounces of herbal therapy product should be added to the juice to get the correct concentration for this batch of product? **(D)**
A) 6
B) 7
C) 11
D) 21

331) A delivery route has rest points marked out at equal intervals. There are 7 rest points on the route, including the rest point at your final destination. It takes $1^1/_4$ hours to travel to the first rest point. The driver is allowed a maximum 15 minute break at each rest point. If the driver travels at a constant speed, how much on-the-road time is needed, excluding time resting, in order to travel to the final destination? **(D)**
A) 7 hours and 15 minutes
B) 7 hours and 45 minutes
C) 8 hours and 45 minutes
D) 10 hours

332) An illusionist has a box of pieces of colored rope for an illusion that he performs at a live show. The box contains 4 pieces of blue rope, 2 pieces of white rope, 1 piece of green rope, 4 pieces of yellow rope, and 5 pieces of black rope. The illusionist selects pieces of rope at random and the first piece of rope he selects is blue. What is the probability that he will select a piece of blue rope again on the second draw? Note that the pieces of rope are not put back into the box once they have been selected. **(A)**

A) $1/_5$ B) $1/_4$ C) $3/_{16}$ D) $4/_{15}$

333) At an elementary school, 3 out of ten students are taking an art class. If the school has 650 students in total, how many total students are taking an art class? **(D)**
A) 65
B) 130
C) 195
D) 217

Look at the information below and answer questions 334 to 336.

The journey on the Regional Railway is always exactly the same duration. The journey from Blairstown to Andersonville is the same duration as the journey from Andersonville to Blairstown.

Regional Railway Train Service from Andersonville to Blairstown	
Departure Time (Andersonville)	Arrival Time (Blairstown)
9:50 am	10:36 am
11:15 am	12:01 pm
12:30 pm	
2:15 pm	3:01 pm
	5:51 pm

334) What is the missing departure time from Andersonville in the chart above? **(E)**
A) 1:16 pm
B) 4:15 pm
C) 4:30 pm
D) 5:05 pm

335) What is the missing arrival time in Blairstown in the chart above? **(E)**
A) 1:16 pm
B) 2:05 pm
C) 2:16 pm
D) 5:05 pm

336) How much travel time, excluding time spent waiting at the station, will it take to travel from Andersonville to Blairstown and back again to Andersonville? **(E)**
A) 46 minutes
B) 1 hour and 22 minutes
C) 1 hour and 32 minutes
D) 2 hours and 32 minutes

Look at the table below and answer questions 337 to 341.

Sunday	Monday	Tuesday	Wednesday	Thursday	Friday	Saturday
−10°F	−9°F	1°F	6°F	8°F	13°F	12°F

337) What was the difference between the temperatures on Sunday and on Saturday? **(E)**
A) 22°
B) 23°
C) 2°
D) −2°

338) What was the median temperature for the week? **(D)**
   A) 1°
   B) 3°
   C) 6°
   D) 22°

339) What was the mean temperature for the week? **(D)**
   A) 1°
   B) 3°
   C) 6°
   D) 22°

340) What was the mode in the temperatures for the week? **(A)**
   A) 1°
   B) 3°
   C) 8°
   D) no mode

341) What is the range in the temperatures for the week? **(D)**
   A) −2°
   B) −3°
   C) −23°
   D) 23°

342) Mustafa bought 4 quarts of cranberry juice for $3 per quart and x quarts of orange juice for $2 per quart. The average cost of both drinks was ($12 + 2x$) ÷ (4 + x). What quantity will be represented at the y intercept of the graph if the equation ($12 + 2x$) ÷ (4 + x) is graphed in the xy plane? **(A)**
   A) 5
   B) 4
   C) 3
   D) 2

343) What term is next in the following sequence?   25, −5, 1, −$1/5$, . . . **(A)**
   A) −$1/25$
   B) $1/25$
   C) −1
   D) 1

344) The speed of sound in a recent experiment was 340,000 millimeters per second. How far did the sound travel in 1,000 seconds? **(A)**
   A) 3.4×10^5 millimeters
   B) 3.4×10^6 millimeters
   C) 3.4×10^7 millimeters
   D) 3.4×10^8 millimeters

345) A is 3 times B, and B is 3 more than 6 times C. Which of the following describes the relationship between A and C? **(A)**
   A) A is 9 more than 18 times C.
   B) A is 3 more than 3 times C.
   C) A is 3 more than 18 times C.
   D) A is 6 more than 3 times C.

346) $x^{-4} = ?$ **(A)**
   A) $4\sqrt{x}$
   B) $\sqrt[-4]{x}$
   C) $x^4 \div 1$
   D) $1 \div x^4$

347) If $5(4\sqrt{x} - 3) = 40$, then $x = ?$ **(D)**
   A) $\frac{5}{12}$
   B) 4
   C) 16
   D) $\sqrt{\frac{5}{12}}$

348) $\sqrt[3]{\frac{8}{27}} = ?$ **(A)**
   A) $\frac{2}{3}$
   B) $\frac{4}{9}$
   C) $\frac{2}{9}$
   D) $\frac{\sqrt{8}}{9}$

349) $-|5-8| = ?$ **(D)**
   A) -13
   B) 13
   C) -3
   D) 3

350) $\sqrt{18} \times \sqrt{8} = ?$ **(D)**
   A) $18\sqrt{8}$
   B) $\sqrt{26}$
   C) $\sqrt{12}$
   D) 12

TABE 9 & 10 Practice Test 5

351) A company measures profits and losses for its four production lines and has recorded the following figures: −14, 52, −36, −7. What was the total profit or loss for all four production lines? **(E)**
A) −23
B) 23
C) 9
D) −5

352) A business has already achieved $9/16$ of its projected sales for this year. Approximately what percentage of the projected sales have already been achieved? **(E)**
A) 0.5625%
B) 5.625%
C) 56.25%
D) 43.75%

353) Employee retention rate is calculated by dividing the number of employees who work for a company at the end of the year into the number of employees who worked for the company at the start of the year. Last year, the employee retention rate was 0.95. What percentage best represents the employee retention rate for last year? **(E)**
A) 0.95%
B) 9.50%
C) 95.0%
D) 950%

354) Employee loss rate is calculated by dividing the number of employees who left a company during the year into the total number of employees in the company at the start of the year. You had 120 employees at the start of the year, and your employee loss rate was 0.05 for the year. How many employees do you have at the end of the year? **(M)**
A) 119
B) 114
C) 12
D) 6

355) A furniture store that sells tables, chairs, and other types of furniture has given a 20 percent discount this month on one of the tables that it sells. This amounts to a discount of $60. What was the original price of the table? **(D)**
A) $80
B) $120
C) $1200
D) $300

356) An ice cream store orders ice cream in 10-quart containers. At the start of the day on Wednesday, there were $6^3/4$ quarts of praline nut ice. At the close of business that Wednesday, there were $2^1/2$ quarts of praline nut ice cream left. How much praline nut ice cream was sold that day? **(M)**
A) $4^1/4$
B) $4^3/8$
C) $4^5/8$
D) $4^6/8$

357) 9 ounces of liquid need to be added to every 6 ounces of active chemical. The current job lot requires 10 ounces of active chemical. How many ounces of liquid should be added? **(D)**
A) 1.50
B) 15.0
C) 0.67
D) 67.0

358) Susan wanted to find the mean of the six surveys she administered this month. However, she erroneously divided the total points from the six surveys by 5, which gave her a result of 96. What is the correct mean of her six surveys? **(A)**
A) 63
B) 80
C) 82
D) 91

359) A bakery makes brownies, cakes, and other confections every day. It allows employees to take home the goods that have not sold by the close of business each day. There are 3 partial trays of unsold brownies at the end of the day, and each tray has $1/8$ of the brownies left in it. These brownies need to be divided among four employees. What amount below represents the fraction of a tray of brownies that each employee will receive? **(A)**
A) $1/6$
B) $32/3$
C) $3/32$
D) $3/24$

360) This month Person A lost $14\frac{3}{4}$ pounds, Person B lost $20\frac{1}{5}$ pounds, and Person C lost 36.35 pounds. What is the total weight loss for these three people? **(M)**
A) 71.30
B) 71.05
C) 71.15
D) 71.25

361) An office purchased 50 reams of paper this month. At the end of the month, 5 of these reams of paper have been used. Which decimal figure below best expresses the amount of reams of paper that have been used in relation to the amount of reams that were purchased? **(M)**
A) 0.0010
B) 0.0100
C) 0.1000
D) 0.0500

362) One hundred prospective candidates took an aptitude test for a new job opening. The 55 female candidates had an average score of 87, while the 45 male candidates had an average of 80. What was the average aptitude test score for all 100 candidates? **(A)**
A) 82.00
B) 83.15
C) 83.50
D) 83.85

363) Mary works for a charity and needs to get $650 in donations. So far, she has obtained 80% of the money she needs. How much money does she still need? **(M)**
A) $130.00
B) $13.00
C) $32.50
D) $81.85

364) The Abdul family is shopping at a superstore. They buy product A and product B. Product A costs $5 each, and product B costs $8 each. They buy 4 of product A. They also buy a certain quantity of product B. The total value of their purchase is $60. How many units of product B did they buy? **(D)**
A) 4
B) 5
C) 6
D) 8

365) The price of socks is $2 per pair and the price of shoes is $25 per pair. Anna went shopping for socks and shoes, and she paid $85 in total. In this purchase, she bought 3 pairs of shoes. How many pairs of socks did she buy? **(A)**
A) 2
B) 3
C) 5
D) 8

366) Chain-link fence is sold by the 1/2 yard. Each 1/2 yard sells for $10.50. One customer buys 20 1/2 yards of this particular type of fence. How much will the customer pay for this purchase? **(D)**
A) $215.25
B) $225.75
C) $430.50
D) $450.50

367) $49^{3}/_{16}$ inches of rope is needed to finish one job and $18^{1}/_{16}$ inches is needed for another. How many inches of rope are needed in order to complete both jobs? **(M)**
A) $66^{1}/_{8}$
B) $67^{1}/_{8}$
C) $66^{1}/_{4}$
D) $67^{1}/_{4}$

368) 11 out of 132 SIM cards are defective. What percentage best represents the amount of defective SIM cards in relation to the total? **(E)**
A) 0.08%
B) 8%
C) 83%
D) 92%

369) To make soda-bread biscuits, the best proportion of baking soda to flour is 2 to 9. A batch of soda-bread biscuits calls for 126 cups of flour. How many cups of baking soda should be used? **(D)**
A) 28
B) 18
C) 14
D) 7

370) Marsha worked from 12:10 PM to 2:25 PM knitting 3 caps by hand from alpaca yarn. At this rate, how many caps will she knit during a 9-hour period? **(D)**
A) 6
B) 12
C) 36
D) 27

371) Market research shows that 58% of your customers are 10 to 20 pounds overweight and 27% of your customers are 21 to 30 pounds overweight. What percentage below represents the amount of customers that are 10 to 30 pounds overweight? **(E)**
   A) 27%
   B) 31%
   C) 75%
   D) 85%

372) If a circle has a radius of 4, what equation can be used to calculate the circumference of the circle? **(A)**
   A) 3.14 ÷ 8
   B) 3.14 ÷ 16
   C) 8 × 3.14
   D) 16 × 3.14

373) If a circle has a radius of 6, what equation can be used to calculate the area of the circle? **(A)**
   A) 6 × 3.14
   B) 12 × 3.14
   C) 24 × 3.14
   D) 36 × 3.14

374) If circle A has a radius of 0.4 and circle B has a radius of 0.2, what is the difference in area between the two circles? **(A)**
   A) 0.1256
   B) 0.3768
   C) 0.5024
   D) 1.256

375) A rectangular box has a base that is 5 inches wide and 6 inches long. The height of the box is 10 inches. What is the volume of the box in cubic inches? **(A)**
   A) 30
   B) 110
   C) 150
   D) 300

376) Find the area of the right triangle whose base is 2 and height is 5. **(D)**
   A) 2.5
   B) 5
   C) 10
   D) 15

377) Find the approximate volume of a cone which has a radius of 3 and a height of 4. **(A)**
   A) 12.56
   B) 37.68
   C) 4.1762
   D) 2.355

378) Pat wants to put wooden trim around the floor of her family room. Each piece of wood is 1 foot in length. The room is rectangular and is 12 feet long and 10 feet wide. How many pieces of wood does Pat need for the entire perimeter of the room? **(A)**
   A) 22
   B) 44
   C) 100
   D) 120

379) The Johnson's have decided to remodel their upstairs. They currently have 4 rooms upstairs that measure 10 feet by 10 feet each. When they remodel, they will make one large room that will be 20 feet by 10 feet and two small rooms that will each be 10 feet by 8 feet. The remaining space is to be allocated to a new bathroom. What are the dimensions of the new bathroom? **(A)**
A) 4 × 10
B) 8 × 10
C) 10 × 10
D) 4 × 8

380) A circular pond has a diameter of 36 feet. What figure below best approximates the area of the pond? **(A)**
A) 1017
B) 804
C) 113
D) 57

381) You need to report the amount of the average high temperature in your town over a three-month period in degrees Fahrenheit. However, the high temperatures are reported in Celsius. You have received the following data: January: 12°C; February: 13°C; March 17°C. What was the average high temperature for these three months in degrees Fahrenheit? °F = 1.8(°C) + 32 **(D)**
A) 57.2
B) 62.6
C) 82.8
D) 25.8

382) A recent report states that 72.8% of the construction for a shopping center is now completed, and it has taken 182 days to do so. If work continues at the same rate, approximately how many more days will be needed to finish the construction? **(D)**
A) 17
B) 18
C) 58
D) 68

Look at the information below and answer questions 383 to 385.

Sam is driving a truck at 70 miles per hour. He will drive through four towns on his route: Brownsville, Dunnstun, Farnam, and Georgetown. At 10:30 am, he sees this sign:

Brownsville	35 miles
Dunnstun	70 miles
Farnam	140 miles
Georgetown	210 miles

383) After Sam sees the sign, he continues to drive at the same speed. At 11:00 am, how far will he be from Farnam? **(M)**
A) He will be in Farnam.
B) He will be 35 miles from Farnam.
C) He will be 70 miles from Farnam.
D) He will be 105 miles from Farnam.

384) Where will Sam be at 12:30 pm? **(M)**
 A) He will be 35 miles past Brownsville.
 B) He will be 70 miles from Farnam.
 C) He will be 70 miles from Georgetown.
 D) He will be 130 miles from Georgetown.

385) What time will Sam arrive in Georgetown if he takes a 30 minute break in Farnam? **(D)**
 A) 1:00 pm
 B) 1:30 pm
 C) 2:00 pm
 D) 2:30 pm

Look at the bar chart below and answer questions 386 to 388.

An athlete ran 10 miles in 1.5 hours. The graph below shows the miles the athlete ran every 10 minutes.

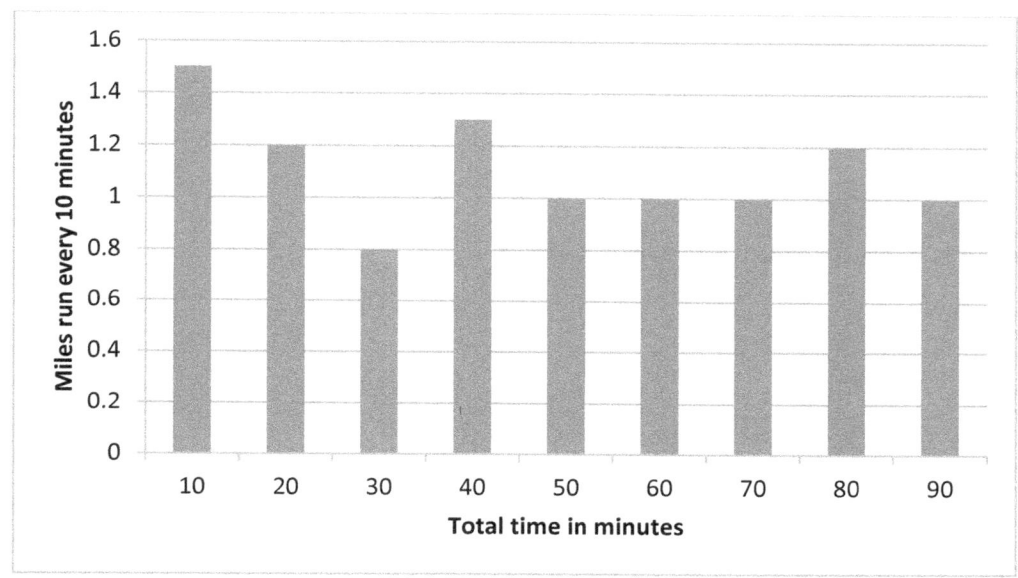

386) According to the graph, about how many miles did the athlete run in the first 30 minutes? **(M)**
 A) 0.8 miles
 B) 2.0 miles
 C) 3.0 miles
 D) 3.5 miles

387) What was the median of the miles the athlete ran every 10 minutes for the entire race? **(D)**
 A) 0.8 mile
 B) 1 mile
 C) 1.2 miles
 D) 1.3 miles

388) What was the range of the miles the athlete ran every 10 minutes for the entire race? **(D)**
 A) 0.7 mile
 B) 0.8 mile
 C) 1 mile
 D) 1.2 miles

Look at the information below and answer questions 389 to 392.

A recipe of the ingredients needed to make 4 brownies is provided below.

> Brownie recipe
>
> ¼ cup of flour
> ½ cup of sugar
> ¼ cup of butter
> 3 tablespoons of cocoa powder
> ¼ teaspoon of baking powder
> ½ teaspoon of vanilla extract

389) How much flour and sugar together is needed to double the above recipe? **(M)**
  A) ¾ cup
  B) 1¼ cups
  C) 1½ cups
  D) 2 cups

390) How much sugar is needed to make 2 brownies? **(M)**
  A) ¼ cup
  B) ¾ cup
  C) 1 cup
  D) 2 cups

391) How much vanilla extract is needed to make 6 brownies? **(D)**
  A) ¼ teaspoon
  B) ¾ teaspoon
  C) 1¼ teaspoons
  D) 1½ teaspoons

392) How much cocoa powder and baking powder together is needed to make 12 brownies?
  (1 tablespoon = 3 teaspoons) **(D)**
  A) 9¼ teaspoons
  B) 27¼ teaspoons
  C) 27½ teaspoons
  D) 27¾ teaspoons

393) A dance judge awards a number from 1 to 10 to score dancers during a TV show. During one show, he judged five dancers and awarded the following scores: 9.9, 9.9, 8.2, 7.6 and 6.8. What was the median value of his scores for this show? **(D)**
  A) 8.2
  B) 8.48
  C) 9.9
  D) 3.1

394) A doctor measures the pulse for several patients one morning. She recorded these results: 54, 68, 62, 60, 75, 58, 84, and 91. What is the range for this group of patients? **(D)**
   A) 30
   B) 37
   C) 65
   D) 69

395) Find the midpoint between the following coordinates: (5, 7) and (11, −3) **(D)**
   A) (2, 5)
   B) (5, 2)
   C) (2, 8)
   D) (8, 2)

396) What number is next in the sequence? 7, 14, 21, 28 **(M)**
   A) 35
   B) 42
   C) 49
   D) 56

397) Evaluate: $2x^2 - x + 5$ if $x = -2$ **(D)**
   A) 8
   B) 13
   C) 15
   D) 20

398) Solve for x: $-6x + 5 = -19$ **(D)**
   A) 4
   B) 6
   C) 8
   D) 12

399) If $2(3x - 1) = 4(x + 1) - 3$, what is the value of x? **(A)**
   A) $3/2$
   B) 3
   C) $2/3$
   D) 2

400) Which of the following expressions is equivalent to $2xy - 8x^2y + 6y^2x^2$? **(D)**
   A) $2(xy - 4x^2y + 3x^2y^2)$
   B) $2xy(-4x + 3xy)$
   C) $2xy(1 - 4x + 3xy)$
   D) $2xy(1 + 4x - 3xy)$

TABE 9 & 10 Practice Tests – Solutions and Explanations

1) The correct answer is C. The problem is asking for the total for all three years, so we add the three figures together: $25,135 + $32,787 + $47,004 = $104,926

2) The correct answer is D. For questions that ask you to calculate the change given to a customer, you need to take the amount of money the customer gives the cashier and subtract the amount of the purchase: $50.00 − $41.28 = $8.72

3) The correct answer is D. Multiplication problems will often include the words 'each' or 'every.' The problem states that the salesperson earns a $175 referral fee on every customer, so the referral fee was earned 8 times this month. We need to multiply the amount of the referral fee by the number of customers to solve: $175 × 8 = $1400

4) The correct answer is C. Division problems will often include the word 'per.' The problem states that the employee works 30 hours per week. So, we divide the total weekly amount by the number of hours to solve: $535.50 ÷ 30 = $17.85

5) The correct answer is B. When you have to add a negative number to a positive number, you are really subtracting. So, add the business profits and subtract the business losses:
953 + 1502 − 286 − 107 = 2062

6) The correct answer is A. In this problem, we need to subtract the excess of the depth of Lake Bajo from the location below sea level of Lake Alto. The location below sea level of Lake Alto is a negative number, so we subtract as follows: −35 − 62 = −97. Remember to express your result as a negative number.

7) The correct answer is B. In order to express a fraction as a decimal, treat the line in the fraction as the division symbol: 3/5 = 3 ÷ 5 = 0.60. Be careful with the decimal placement in your final result.

8) The correct answer is C. To express a decimal number as a percent, move the decimal point two places to the right and add the percent sign: 0.55 = 55.0%

9) The correct answer is D. In order to express a fraction as a percentage, you need to divide and then express the result as a percentage. Step 1 – Treat the line in the fraction as the division symbol: 5/14 = 5 ÷ 14 = 0.357. Step 2 – To express the result from Step 1 as a percentage, we need to move the decimal point two places to the right and add the percent sign: 0.357 = 35.7%

10) The correct answer is D. For your exam, you should be able to recognize the equivalent fractions for commonly-used decimal numbers. If you are unsure, perform division on the answer choices to check:
3/4 = 3 ÷ 4 = 0.75

11) The correct answer is A. For your exam, you should be able to recognize the equivalent fractions for commonly-used percentages. If you are unsure, perform division on the answer choices to check:
1/3 = 1 ÷ 3 = 0.3333 = 33%

12) The correct answer is C. Any given percentage is out of 100%, so we divide by 100 to express a percentage as a decimal. So, move the decimal point two places to the left and remove the percent sign:
45% = 45 ÷ 100 = 0.45

13) The correct answer is B. Express both amounts as decimal numbers and multiply to solve: $14\frac{1}{4}$ pounds × 36 cents per pound = 14.25 × 0.36 = $5.13

14) The correct answer is C. There are 60 minutes in an hour, so multiply the minutes in the hour by the decimal number given in the problem to solve: 60 minutes × 0.35 hour = 60 × 0.35 = 21 minutes

15) The correct answer is A. Step 1 – Subtract the discount from the original price: $24 – $5 = $19. Step 2 – Take the result from Step 1 and multiply by the number of units sold: $19 × 12 = $228

16) The correct answer is D. Step 1 – Determine the total number of hours worked: 7 hours per day for 4 days = 7 × 4 = 28 hours. Step 2 – Calculate the profit the company makes per hour. The customer was billed $45 per hour for the employee's work, and he was paid $25 per hour: $45 – $25 = $20 profit per hour. Step 3 – Multiply the total number of hours by the profit per hour to solve: 28 hours × $20 profit per hour 28 × 20 = $560

17) The correct answer is A. Step 1 – Calculate how many minutes there are in 40 hours: 40 hours × 60 minutes per hour = 2400 minutes. Step 2 – Divide the amount of prescriptions into the previous result to get the rate: 2400 ÷ 250 = 9.6 minutes per prescription

18) The correct answer is C. The orders that were delivered on time are part of the total order. So, take the amount of orders that were delivered on time and divide by the amount of total orders: 105 ÷ 120 = 0.875 = 87.5%

19) The correct answer is B. On Monday cell growth was 27, and for all of the days Tuesday through Friday, cell attrition was 13 per day. Step 1 – Cell attrition is a negative number, so perform multiplication to get the total for the four days (Tuesday through Friday): –13 × 4 = –52. Step 2 – On Monday cell growth was 27, so add this to the result from Step 1 to solve: –52 + 27 = –25

20) The correct answer is B. To find the average, you need to find the total, and then divide the total by the number of hours. Step 1 – Find the total: 23 + 25 + 26 + 24 + 22 = 120. Step 2 – Divide the result from Step 1 by the number of hours: 120 ÷ 5 = 24

21) The correct answer is D. Step 1 – Take the 66 units of cement powder for the current batch and divide by the 3 units stated in the original ratio: 22 ÷ 3 = 22. Step 2 – Multiply the result from Step 1 by the 2 units of sand stated in the original ratio to get your answer: 2 × 22 = 44

22) The correct answer is D. The problem states that we are working with a ratio, so the employees and the supervisors form separate groups. Step 1 – Add the two groups together: 50 + 1 = 51. Step 2 – Take the total amount of employees stated in the problem and divide this by the figure calculated in Step 1 to get the amount of supervisors: 255 ÷ 51 = 5

23) The correct answer is D. The problem uses the phrase '2 out of every 20 employees' so we know that there are 2 employees who form a subset within each group of 20. Step 1 – Take the total number of employees and divide this by 20: 480 ÷ 20 = 24. Step 2 – Take the result from Step 1 and multiply by the amount in the subset to solve: 24 × 2 = 48

24) The correct answer is C. Step 1 – Calculate the amount of time spent on the initial job to do 3 wheel covers: 8:10 to 8:22 = 12 minutes. Step 2 – Calculate how many minutes are needed to change 1 wheel cover: 12 minutes ÷ 3 = 4 minutes each. Step 3 – Divide the figure from Step 2 into 60 minutes to solve: 60 ÷ 4 = 15

25) The correct answer is C. Step 1 – Add the whole numbers. The whole numbers are the numbers in front of the fractions: 15 + 13 = 28. Step 2 – Add the fractions. If you have two fractions that have the same denominator, you add the numerators and keep the common denominator: 2/8 + 5/8 = 7/8.

Step 3 – Combine the results from Step 1 and Step 2 to get your new mixed number to solve the problem: 28 + 7/8 = 28⁷/₈

26) The correct answer is A. Step 1 – Add the whole numbers: 2 + 4 = 6. Step 2 – Add the fractions. If you have two fractions that have the same denominator, you add the numerators and keep the common denominator: 1/8 + 3/8 = 4/8. Step 3 – Simplify the fraction from Step 2: 4/8 = (4 ÷ 4)/(8 ÷ 4) = 1/2. Step 4 – Combine the results from Step 1 and Step 3 to get your new mixed number to solve the problem: 6 + 1/2 = 6½

27) The correct answer is A. Step 1 – Subtract the whole numbers: 5 – 4 = 1. Step 2 – Subtract the fractions. If you have two fractions that have the same denominator, you subtract the numerators and keep the common denominator: 3/16 – 1/16 = 2/16. Step 3 – Simplify the fraction from Step 2: 2/16 = (2 ÷ 2)/(16 ÷ 2) = 1/8. Step 4 – Combine the results from Step 1 and Step 3 to get your new mixed number to solve the problem: 1 + 1/8 = 1¹/₈

28) The correct answer is B. Add the three figures together to solve: 0.25 + 0.50 + 0.10 = 0.85. Remember to be sure to put the decimal point in the correct place when you work out the solution to problems like this one.

29) The correct answer is C. Add the percentages together to solve: 25% + 50% = 75%

30) The correct answer is D. Step 1 – Multiply the whole numbers: 5 × 1 = 5. Step 2 – Multiply the whole number by the fraction: 5 × 1/4 = 5/4. Step 3 – Convert the fraction from Step 2 to a mixed number: 5/4 = 1¹/₄. Step 4 – Combine the results from Step 1 and Step 3 to get your new mixed number: 5 + 1¹/₄ = 6¹/₄. Step 5 – Convert the result from Step 4 to hours and minutes: 6¹/₄ hours = 6 hours and 15 minutes

31) The correct answer is B. Step 1 – Convert the first fraction to the common denominator: 1/8 = (1 × 4)/(8 × 4) = 4/32. Step 2 – Add one more increment to this to get your result: 4/32 + 1/32 = 5/32

32) The correct answer is A. Step 1 – Work out the cost for the first supplier: 50 units × $0.50 = $25. Step 2 – Compare to other deals to solve: The other deals are $27.50 and $30, so $25 is the best deal.

33) The correct answer is D. Step 1 – Determine the duration of the stay in weeks and nights: 9 nights = 1 week + 2 nights. Step 2 – Add the cost for 1 week to the cost for 2 days to solve: $280 + (2 × $45) = $280 + $90 = $370

34) The correct answer is D. Step 1 – Determine the dollar value of the discount: $15 – $12 = $3. Step 2 – Divide the result from Step 1 by the original price to get the percentage: $3 ÷ $15 = 0.20 = 20%

35) The correct answer is C. Step 1 – Determine the dollar value of the markup on the mug: $9 retail price – $3 cost = $6 markup. Step 2 – Calculate the percentage of the markup by dividing the dollar value of the markup by the cost: $6 ÷ $3 = 2.00 = 200%. Step 3 – Use the percentage markup from the previous step to determine the dollar value of the markup on the bowl: $4 × 200% = $4 × 2 = $8. Step 4 – Add the dollar value of the markup for the bowl to the cost of the bowl to get the retail price: $8 + $4 = $12

36) The correct answer is D. To calculate a reverse percentage you need to divide, rather than multiply. So, take the $20 discount and divide by the 25% percentage: $20 ÷ 25% = $20 ÷ 0.25 = $80

37) The correct answer is C. Step 1 – Add the times for the first two processes and express in terms of hours and minutes: Production time of 3 hours and 25 minutes + Bottling and labeling time of 1 hour and 40 minutes = 3 hours + 1 hour + 25 minutes + 40 minutes = 4 hours and 65 minutes = 5 hours and 5 minutes. Step 2 – Add the time for the packaging process of 26 hours to the result from Step 1: 5 hours and 5 minutes + 26 hours = 31 hours and 5 minutes. Step 3 – Determine the time that the batch will be ready for shipment. 31 hours and 5 minutes have passed. In other words, a period of 24 hours and an additional 7 hours and 5 minutes have passed. The process started on Monday at 10:30 am, so by

Tuesday at 10:30 am, 24 hours will have passed. An additional 7 hours and 5 minutes takes us to Tuesday at 5:35 pm.

38) The correct answer is C. Step 1 – Determine the cost from the first supplier: 240 × 0.25 = $60. The tax on this will be $60 × 6.5% = $60 × 0.065 = $3.90. Then add the tax to the cost to get the total: $60 + $3.90 = $63.90. Step 2 – Determine the total cost from the second supplier: $58 cost + ($58 × 0.065 tax) = $58 + 3.77 = $61.77. So, you will get the better deal from the second supplier at $61.77.

39) The correct answer is D. Step 1 – Determine how many days are needed to make the small frames. 20 small frames can be made in 4 days: 20 frames ÷ 4 days = 5 small frames per day. The customer wants 40 small frames, so divide by the rate to determine how many days are going to be needed for the small frames: 40 frames ÷ 5 per day = 8 days. Step 2 – Determine how many days are going to be needed to make the large frames. 21 larges frames can be made in 3 days: 21 ÷ 3 = 7 large frames per day. 64 large frames need to be made for the order: 64 ÷ 7 = 9.1 days. Step 3 – Add the results from the two previous steps to solve: 8 days + 9.1 days = 17.1 days, which we round down to 17 days.

40) The correct answer is C. Step 1 – Calculate the percentage of work completed per day. 12.5% of the work has been completed in 4 days: 12.5 % ÷ 4 days = 3.125% per day. Step 2 – Determine how many days in total are needed to complete the entire job by dividing 100% by the result from the previous step: 100% ÷ 3.125% = 32 days. Step 3 – Determine the number of days remaining: 32 days in total – 4 days completed = 28 days remaining

41) The correct answer is B. From the formula, we can see that 1 foot = 0.3048 meters. To solve, multiply the amount of 538 feet, stated in the question, by 0.3048: 538 × 0.3048 = 163.98, which we round up to 164.

42) The correct answer is D. Step 1 – Add the feet together: 123 + 138 = 261 feet. Step 2 – Add the inches together: 6 + 8 = 14 inches. Step 3 – Convert the inches to feet and inches if the result from Step 2 is 12 inches or more: 14 inches = 1 foot 2 inches. Step 4 – Combine the results from Step 1 and Step 3 to solve: 261 feet + 1 foot 2 inches = 262 feet 2 inches

43) The correct answer is A. Step 1 – Convert the weight of the full box from pounds and ounces to just ounces. We are using the formula 1 pound = 16 ounces, so 8 pounds and 5 ounces = (8 × 16) + 5 = 128 + 5 = 133 ounces. Step 2 – The problem states that the box weighs 7 ounces when it is empty. So, subtract the weight of the empty box from the weight of the full box to get the weight of the product inside the box: 133 ounces – 7 ounces = 126 ounces. Step 3 – The problem tells us that each supplement weighs 0.75 ounces. Take the total weight from the previous step and divide by the weight per unit to determine how many units the box contains: 126 ounces ÷ 0.75 ounces = 168 units

44) The correct answer is B. Step 1 – Convert the mixed numbers to decimals and then multiply: 50¼ feet × 60¼ feet = 50.25 × 60.25 = 3027.5625 square feet. Step 2 – The price is given in square yards, so convert the square feet from the previous step to square yards. The formula states that 1 square yard = 9 square feet, so 1/9 square yard = 1 square foot: 3027.5625 square feet ÷ 9 = 336.3958 square yards. Step 3 – Calculate the cost: 336.3958 × $5.25 = $1765.92, which we round to $1,766.

45) The correct answer is B. Step 1 – Calculate the amount of remaining stock in inches: (2 × 75 inches) + (4 × 25.25 inches) = 150 + 101 = 251 inches. Step 2 – Convert the existing stock from inches to yards: 1 foot = 12 inches and 1 yard = 3 feet, so there are 36 inches in 1 yard. So, divide the amount of inches by 36 to convert to yards: 251 ÷ 36 = 6.97 yards. Step 3 – Calculate the amount required to restock. 60 yards are required in total, and there are 6.97 yards on hand, so subtract to find out how many more yards are needed to get the stock back up to 60 yards: 60 – 6.97 = 53.03 yards needed. Step 4 – The yarn comes in 5-yard balls, so calculate how many balls to buy to cover the 53.03 yards that are required: 53.03 ÷ 5 = 10.6 balls. It is not possible to buy a fractional part of a ball, so we round up to 11 balls.

46) The correct answer is D. Step 1 – Convert 0.75 grams to milligrams. 1 gram = 1,000 milligrams, so 0.75 grams × 1,000 = 750 milligrams. Step 2 – The normal ratio is in the amount of 50 milligrams, so

divide the result from the previous step by 50: 750 ÷ 50 = 15. So, 15 times more active ingredient is being used than normal. Step 3 – Determine the amount of liquid. Since 15 times more of the active ingredient is being used, we also need to use 15 times more of the liquid: 1.5 milliliters × 15 = 22.5 milliliters

47) The correct answer is A. Our points are (5, 2) and (7, 4), so substitute the values into the midpoint formula.
$(x_1 + x_2) ÷ 2$, $(y_1 + y_2) ÷ 2$
(5 + 7) ÷ 2 = midpoint x, (2 + 4) ÷ 2 = midpoint y
12 ÷ 2 = midpoint x, 6 ÷ 2 = midpoint y
6 = midpoint x, 3 = midpoint y

48) The correct answer is B. First, find the midpoint of the x coordinates for (**−4**, 2) and (**8**,−6).
midpoint $x = (x_1 + x_2) ÷ 2$
midpoint x = (−4 + 8) ÷ 2
midpoint x = 4 ÷ 2
midpoint x = 2
Then find the midpoint of the y coordinates for (−4, **2**) and (8,**−6**).
midpoint $y = (y_1 + y_2) ÷ 2$
midpoint y = (2 + −6) ÷ 2
midpoint y = −4 ÷ 2
midpoint y = −2
So, the midpoint is (2, −2)

49) The correct answer is D. Substitute the values (2, 3) and (6, 7) into the formula.
$d = \sqrt{(x_2 - x_1)^2 + (y_2 - y_1)^2}$
$d = \sqrt{(6 - 2)^2 + (7 - 3)^2}$
$d = \sqrt{4^2 + 4^2}$
$d = \sqrt{16 + 16}$
$d = \sqrt{32}$

50) The correct answer is A. Substitute the values into the slope-intercept formula.
y = mx + b
315 = m5 + 15
315 − 15 = m5 + 15 − 15
300 = m5
300 ÷ 5 = m5 ÷ 5
60 = m

51) The correct answer is A. As y increases by 5, x decreases by 5. So, the slope is −1. The line includes point (20, 15), which is the fifth point from the left.

52) The correct answer is A. Remember that the y intercept is where the line crosses the y axis, so x = 0 for the y intercept. Begin by substituting 0 for x.
y = x + 14
y = 0 + 14
y = 14
Therefore, the coordinates (0, 14) represent the y intercept.

On the other hand, the x intercept exists where the line crosses the x axis, so y = 0 for the x intercept. Now substitute 0 for y.
y = x + 14
0 = x + 14
0 − 14 = x + 14 − 14
−14 = x
So, the coordinates (−14, 0) represent the x intercept.

53) The correct answer is A. The x intercept is the point at which a line crosses the x axis of a graph. In order for the line to cross the x axis, y must be equal to zero at that particular point of the graph. On the other hand, the y intercept is the point at which the line crosses the y axis. So, in order for the line to cross the y axis, x must be equal to zero at that particular point of the graph. First, substitute 0 for y in order to find the x intercept.
$x^2 + 2y^2 = 144$
$x^2 + (2 \times 0) = 144$
$x^2 + 0 = 144$
$x^2 = 144$
$x = 12$
Then substitute 0 for x in order to find the y intercept.
$x^2 + 2y^2 = 144$
$(0 \times 0) + 2y^2 = 144$
$0 + 2y^2 = 144$
$2y^2 \div 2 = 144 \div 2$
$y^2 = 72$
$y = \sqrt{72}$
So, the y intercept is $(0, \sqrt{72})$ and the x intercept is (12, 0).

54) The correct answer is B. From the formula, we can see that the area of a triangle is ½ (base × height). So, substitute the values to solve: ½ (base × height) = ½ (12 × 14) = ½ × 168 = 84 square inches

55) The correct answer is C. Use the Pythagorean Theorem to solve. $C = \sqrt{A^2 + B}$
$C = \sqrt{A^2 + B^2} = \sqrt{3^2 + 2^2} = \sqrt{9 + 4} = \sqrt{13}$

56) The correct answer is C. The sum of the angles in a triangle is 180 degrees. So, subtract the measurements of the other two angles to solve: 180° − 47° − 44° = 89°

57) The correct answer is D. From the tip after the question, we can see that a circle has 360 degrees. So, subtract to solve: 360 − 82 − 79 − 46 − 85 = 68

58) The correct answer is A. From the formula, we can see that the area of a circle ≈ 3.14 × (radius)². So, put in 12 feet for the radius to solve: 3.14 × (12 × 12) = 3.14 × 144 = 452.16

59) The correct answer is C. From the formula, we know that the circumference of a circle ≈ 3.14 × diameter. The problem states that the diameter of the tractor tire is 46.5 inches, so use that in the formula to solve: 3.14 × 46.5 = 146.01 inches

60) The correct answer is D. The area of a rectangle = length × width. Your quilt is 6 feet long and 5 feet wide, so multiply to solve: 6 × 5 = 30

61) The correct answer is B. The perimeter of a rectangle = 2(length + width). Your field is 12 yards long and 9 yards wide, so use the formula to solve: 2(12 + 9) = 2 × 21 = 42

62) The correct answer is B. Step 1 – The area of a circle ≈ 3.14 × radius². Here, we are given the area, so we have to divide by 3.14, instead of multiplying by 3.14, as stated in the formula: 78.5 ÷ 3.14 = 25. Step 2 – The result from the previous step is the radius squared. A squared number is the result of a number that has been multiplied by itself. 5 × 5 = 25, so the length of the radius of the pond is 5 feet. Step 3 – Remember that diameter is double the radius, so if the radius is 5, the diameter is 10 feet.

63) The correct answer is A. For questions on rearranging formulas like this one and the previous one, it is very likely that you are going to have to divide the largest number in the question by a smaller number in order to solve the problem. From the formula, we know that the area of a rectangle = length × width. Here, we are given the area (the larger number of 360), so we need to divide that by the length (the smaller number of 30 feet) in order to get the width: 360 ÷ 30 = 12 feet

64) The correct answer is D. The volume of a rectangular solid = length × width × height. The tank is 5 feet wide, 8 feet long, and 3 feet high, so multiply to solve: 5 × 8 × 3 = 120

65) The correct answer is A. A cube is a three-dimensional object in which all sides have the same length. The volume of a cube = side length³. So, put the length of the side in the formula to solve: 18 × 18 × 18 = 5832

66) The correct answer is A. Step 1 – Calculate in cubic inches the volume of the sphere when it is full. The tank is 72 inches across on the inside, so the radius is 36 inches. The volume of a sphere ≈ 4/3 × 3.14 × radius³: 4/3 × 3.14 × 36³ = 195,333.12 cubic inches. Step 2 – Calculate in cubic inches how much milk remains in the sphere. The tank is now 80% full of milk: 195,333.12 cubic inches × 0.80 = 156,266.50 cubic inches, which we round to 156,267 cubic inches.

67) The correct answer is B. The volume of a cylinder ≈ 3.14 × height × radius². Your tank has a 5 meter radius and is 21 meters in height: 3.14 × 21 × 5² = 3.14 × 21 × 25 = 1648.50 cubic meters

68) The correct answer is C. Step 1 – Calculate the volume of the large cone. The large cones are 6 inches high and have a 1.5 inch radius. The volume of a cone ≈ (3.14 × height × radius²) ÷ 3 = (3.14 × 6 × 1.5 × 1.5) ÷ 3 = 14.13. Step 2 – Calculate the volume of the medium cone. The medium cones are 5 inches high and have a 1 inch radius: (3.14 × height × radius²) ÷ 3 = (3.14 × 5 × 1 × 1) ÷ 3 = 5.23. Step 3 – Calculate the difference between the volume of the two cones: 14.13 – 5.23 = 8.90

69) The correct answer is D. Step 1 – Calculate the dimensions of the floor in inches: 8 feet × 12 inches per foot = 96 inches long; 4 feet × 12 inches in a foot = 48 inches wide. Step 2 – Determine how many wooden pieces will fit along the length of the floor. If we lay the 12-inch side of the wooden piece against the length of the room, we can lay 8 of these side by side to cover the 96-inch length: 96 ÷ 12 = 8. Step 3 – Determine how many wooden pieces can fit along the width. 48-inch-wide floor ÷ 6-inch-wide pieces = 48 ÷ 6 = 8 pieces. Step 4 – Multiply the results from steps 2 and 3 to get the total number of pieces needed for the job: 8 × 8 = 64

70) The correct answer is C. Area of a rectangle = length × width. The wall is 16 feet by 11 feet, so multiply to solve: 16 × 11 = 176

71) The correct answer is A. We know that the volume of a rectangular solid = length × width × height. Here, we are given the volume, so we need to divide that by the length and then the width in order to find the height: (1080 ÷ 12) ÷ 9 = 90 ÷ 9 = 10 feet

72) The correct answer is B. Step 1 – Find the volume in terms of cubic inches. Remember that radius is half of diameter. Here we have a diameter of 12, so the radius is 6. Cylinder volume ≈ 3.14 × radius² ×

height ≈ 3.14 × 6² × 18 ≈ 3.14 × 36 × 18 ≈ 2034.72. Step 2 – Convert the volume in cubic inches to gallons. 1 gallon = 231 cubic inches, so divide by 231 to convert to gallons: 2034.72 ÷ 231 = 8.8 gallons

73) The correct answer is D. Step 1 – First we need to calculate the volume in terms of cubic feet. The volume of a cube = (length of side)³. The length of the side is 9 feet, so the volume is 9 × 9 × 9 = 729 cubic feet. Step 2 – We have to convert the result from Step 1 to cubic inches. From the formula, we can see that 1 cubic foot = 1,728 cubic inches, so multiply to solve: 729 × 1,728 = 1,259,712 cubic inches

74) The correct answer is A. Step 1 – Calculate in cubic feet the volume of the container when it is full. The container is 25 feet long, 12 feet wide and 18 feet high. To find the volume of a rectangular solid, we use the formula: length × width × height = 25 × 12 × 18 = 5,400 cubic feet. Step 2 – Calculate in cubic feet how much product is in the container. The container is now 75% full: 5,400 cubic feet × 0.75 = 4,050 cubic feet. Step 3 – Convert the cubic feet to yards. 1 cubic yard = 27 cubic feet. The formula is cubic yards to cubic feet, but you are converting from cubic feet to cubic yards, so you need to divide: 4,050 cubic feet ÷ 27 = 150 cubic yards

75) The correct answer is C. Step 1 – Calculate the amount of remaining stock in quarts and ounces: [2 × (16 cups and 7 ounces)] + [3 × (20 cups and 4 ounces)] = 32 cups and 14 ounces + 60 cups and 12 ounces = 92 cups and 26 ounces. Step 2 – Convert the existing stock from cups to quarts: 1 quart = 4 cups, so divide the amount of cups by 4 to convert to quarts: (92 cups ÷ 4) + 26 ounces = 23 quarts and 26 ounces. There are 32 ounces in a quart, so we cannot convert the remaining 26 ounces to quarts. Step 3 – Calculate the amount required to restock. 50 quarts are required in total, and you have approximately 23 quarts on hand, so subtract to find out how many more quarts you need to get the stock back up to 50 quarts: 50 – 23 = 27 quarts needed. Step 4 – The chemical comes in 5-quart containers, so calculate how many containers you need to buy to cover the 27 quarts that are required: 27 ÷ 5 = 5.4 quarts. It is not possible to buy a fractional part of a container, so you have to buy 6 containers.

76) The correct answer is D. Step 1 – Calculate the volume of each vat: length × width × height = 10 × 10 × 12 = 1,200 cubic feet. Step 2 – Determine how full each vat is in terms of cubic feet. Vat 1: 1,200 × ³/₄ = 1,200 × 0.75 = 900 cubic feet. Vat 2: 1,200 × ⁴/₅ = 1,200 × 0.80 = 960 cubic feet. Step 3 – Add the volume of the two vats together to determine the total volume: 900 + 960 = 1,860 cubic feet. Step 4 – Convert the cubic feet to cubic inches. 1 cubic foot = 1,728 cubic inches, so we multiply to convert: 1,860 cubic feet × 1,728 = 3,214,080 cubic inches. Step 5 – Multiply by the price to solve: 3,214,080 cubic inches × $0.12 = $385,689.60, which we round to $385,690.

77) The correct answer is B. Step 1 – Calculate the radius of the cone. The diameter is 6 and radius is half of diameter, so the radius is 3. Step 2 – Calculate the correct volume of the cone. The formula for the volume of a cone ≈ (3.14 × radius² × height) ÷ 3 = (3.14 × 3² × 8) ÷ 3 = 226.08 ÷ 3 = 75.36 cubic feet. Step 3 – Compare the correct figure to the erroneous figure to determine whether the erroneous calculation was too large or too small. You calculated 226 cubic feet, so you erred on the large side. Step 4 – Identify where the error occurred. We can see from the calculation in step 2 that final part of the calculation of the volume is (3.14 × 3² × 8) ÷ 3 = 226.08 ÷ 3, so you have forgotten to divide by 3.

78) The correct answer is B. No lights are to be installed in the corners, so each of the two 10-feet walls will have 1 light installed in the middle of each wall: 10 ÷ 5 = 2, but we subtract 1 from this for the corner. So, we have 1 light on each of the 2 shorter walls, which accounts for 2 lights so far. Each of the 25-foot walls have 5 increments of 5 feet, and again no lights are in the corners: (25 ÷ 5) – 1 = 4. So, each of the 2 long walls will have 4 lights on each wall. So there will be 10 lights in total on the walls in the room (1 + 1 + 4 + 4 = 10). You may wish to draw a diagram on your scratch paper when solving problems like this one.

79) The correct answer is D. Step 1 – Calculate the volume of the large ice cube: (1.8 × 1.8 × 1.8) = 5.832. Step 2 – Calculate the volume of the small ice cube: (1.4 × 1.4 × 1.4) = 2.744. Step 3 – Calculate the difference between the volume of the two ice cubes: 5.832 – 2.744 = 3.088

80) The correct answer is D. Step 1 – Calculate the area of the large triangle: (12 × 18) ÷ 2 = 216 ÷ 2 = 108. Step 2 – Calculate the area of the small triangle: (8 × 14) ÷ 2 = 112 ÷ 2 = 56. Step 3 – Subtract to solve: 108 – 56 = 52

81) The correct answer is D. To find the mean, add up all of the items in the set and then divide by the number of items in the set. Here we have 7 numbers in the set, so we get our answer as follows: (89 + 65 + 75 + 68 + 82 + 74 + 86) ÷ 7 = 539 ÷ 7 = 77

82) The correct answer is A. The mode is the number that occurs the most frequently in the set. Our data set is: 1, 1, 3, 2, 4, 3, 1, 2, 1. The number 1 occurs 4 times in the set, which is more frequently than any other number in the set, so the mode is 1.

83) The correct answer is B. The problem provides the number set: 8.19, 7.59, 8.25, 7.35, 9.10
First of all, put the numbers in ascending order: 7.35, 7.59, 8.19, 8.25, 9.10. Then find the one that is in the middle: 7.35, 7.59, **8.19**, 8.25, 9.10

84) The correct answer is A. Put the numbers is ascending order: 2, 2, 3, 5, **6**, **8**, 8, 10, 12, 21. Here, we have got an even number of items, so we need to take an average of the two items in the middle: (8 + 6) ÷ 2 = 7

85) The correct answer is C. To calculate the range, the low number in the set is deducted from the high number in the set. The problem set is: 98.5, 85.5, 80.0, 97, 93, 92.5, 93, 87, 88, 82. The high number is 98.5 and the low number is 80, so the range is 18.5 (98.5 – 80 = 18.5).

86) The correct answer is D. The mode is the number that occurs most frequently. However, if no number occurs more than once, the set has no mode.

87) The correct answer is B. We don't know the age of the 10th car, so put this in as x to solve:
(2 + 3 + 4 + 5 + 6 + 7 + 9 + 10 + 12 + x) ÷ 10 = 6
[(2 + 3 + 4 + 5 + 6 + 7 + 9 + 10 + 12 + x) ÷ 10] × 10 = 6 × 10
2 + 3 + 4 + 5 + 6 + 7 + 9 + 10 + 12 + x = 60
58 + x = 60
x = 2

88) The correct answer is A. Find the total points for the first group: 50 × 82 = 4100. Then find the total points for the second group. 50 × 89 = 4450. Add these two amounts together for the total points: 4100 + 4450 = 8550. Then divide the total points by the total number of members in the group: 8550 ÷ 100 = 85.5

89) The correct answer is C. First, multiply the erroneous average by the erroneous number of tests to get the total points: 78 × 8 = 624. Then divide this total by the correct amount: 624 ÷ 10 = 62.4

90) The correct answer is A. Find the total of the items in the sample space: 5 + 10 + 8 + 12 = 35. We want to know the chance of getting an orange balloon, so put that in the denominator: $\frac{10}{35} = \frac{2}{7}$

91) The correct answer is D. We have 54 cards in the deck (13 × 4 = 52). We have taken out two spades, one heart, and a club, thereby removing 4 cards. So, the available data set is 48 (52 – 4 = 48). The desired outcome is drawing a heart. We have 13 hearts to begin with and one has been removed, so there are 12 hearts left. So, the probability of drawing a heart is $^{12}/_{48} = ^{1}/_{4}$

92) The correct answer is A. To solve problems like this one, it is usually best to write out the possible outcomes in a list. This will help you visualize the number of possible outcomes that make up the sample space. Then circle or highlight the events from the list to get your answer. In this case, we have two

items, each of which has a variable outcome. There are 6 numbers on the black die and 6 numbers on the red die. Using multiplication, we can see that there are 36 possible combinations: 6 × 6 = 36
To check your answer, you can list the possibilities of the various combinations:

(1,1)   (1,2)   (1,3)   (1,4)   (1,5)   (1,6)
(2,1)   (2,2)   (2,3)   (2,4)   (2,5)   (2,6)
(3,1)   (3,2)   (3,3)   (3,4)   (3,5)   (3,6)
(4,1)   (4,2)   (4,3)   (4,4)   (4,5)   (4,6)
(5,1)   (5,2)   (5,3)   **(5,4)**   (5,5)   (5,6)
(6,1)   (6,2)   (6,3)   (6,4)   (6,5)   (6,6)

If the number on the left in each set of parentheses represents the black die and the number on the right represents the red die, we can see that there is one chance that Sam will roll a 4 on the red die and a 5 on the black die. The result is expressed as a fraction, with the event (chance of the desired outcome) in the numerator and the total sample space (total data set) in the denominator. So, the answer is $1/36$.

93) The correct answer is D. You need to determine the amount of possible outcomes at the start of the day first of all. The owner has 10 brown teddy bears, 8 white teddy bears, 4 black teddy bears, and 2 pink teddy bears when she opens the attraction at the start of the day. So, at the start of the day, she has 24 teddy bears: 10 + 8 + 4 + 2 = 24. Then you need to reduce this amount by the quantity of items that have been removed. The problem tells us that she has given out a brown teddy bear, so there are 23 teddy bears left in the sample space: 24 − 1 = 23. The event is the chance of the selection of a pink teddy bear. We know that there are two pink teddy bears left after the first prize winner receives his or her prize. Finally, we need to put the event (the number representing the chance of the desired outcome) in the numerator and the number of possible remaining combinations (the sample space) in the denominator. So the answer is $2/23$.

94) The correct answer is C. Cobb County is the darkest bar, so it is the first bar for each month. For July, Cobb County had 1.2 inches of rain, and in August it had 0.8 inches, so it had 2 inches in total for the two months.

95) The correct answer is B. In June, Dawson County had 1.1 inches of rain and Emery County had 1.7 inches. Therefore, Emery County had 0.6 more inches of rainfall than Dawson County.

96) The correct answer is A. Emery County had the following amounts of rainfall: May = 2.5 inches; June = 1.8 inches; July = 1 inch; August = 0.9 inch. Then add these amounts together to solve: 2.5 + 1.8 + 1 + 0.9 = 6.2 inches in total

97) The correct answer is A. We already know that Emery County had 6.2 total inches of rainfall for the four months from our previous answer. So, add up the four months for Cobb County and then do the same for Dawson County. Cobb County: May = 2.9 inches; June = 2.1 inches; July = 1.2 inches; August 0.8 inches = 7 total inches. Dawson County: May = 3.5 inches; June = 1.1 inches; July = 0.9 inches; August = 2.3 inches = 7.8 total inches. Therefore, Emery County had the lowest total with 6.2 inches.

98) The correct answer is D. Reptiles account for 42% of the zoo creatures at the start of the year, and there are 1,500 creatures in total, so multiply to solve: 1,500 × 0.42 = 630 reptiles

99) The correct answer is B. At the start of the year, 26% of the zoo creatures were quadrupeds and 15% of the creatures were fish. So, solve by multiplying and subtracting as follows: (1500 × 0.26) − (1500 × 0.15) = 390 − 225 = 165 more quadrupeds than fish

100) The correct answer is C. We have to calculate the percentage of birds at the start of the year by subtracting the percentages for the other categories: 100% − 40% − 21% − 16% = 23%. The percentage of birds was 17% at the start of the year and 23% at the end of the year, so there was a 6% increase in the bird population. We can then multiply to solve: 1,500 × 0.06 = 90 more birds at the end of the year

101) The correct answer is C. Substitute –2 for x to solve.
$2x^2 – x + 5 =$
$[2 \times (–2^2)] – (–2) + 5 =$
$[2 \times (4)] – (–2) + 5 =$
$(2 \times 4) + 2 + 5 =$
$8 + 2 + 5 = 15$

102) The correct answer is B. Isolate x to solve. You do this by doing the same operation on each side of the equation.
$–6x + 5 = –19$
Subtract 5 from each side to get rid of the integer 5 on the left side.
$–6x + 5 – 5 = –19 – 5$
Then simplify.
$–6x = –24$
Then divide each side by –6 to isolate x.
$–6x \div –6 = –24 \div –6$
$x = –24 \div –6$
$x = 4$

103) The correct answer is B.
Remember to do multiplication on the items in parentheses first.
$4x – 3(x + 2) = –3$
$4x – 3x – 6 = –3$
Then deal with the integers.
$4x – 3x – 6 + 6 = –3 + 6$
$4x – 3x = 3$
Then solve for x.
$4x – 3x = 3$
$x = 3$

104) The correct answer is C. Isolate the integers to one side of the equation.

$\frac{3}{4}x - 2 = 4$

$\frac{3}{4}x - 2 + 2 = 4 + 2$

$\frac{3}{4}x = 6$

Then get rid of the fraction by multiplying both sides by the denominator.

$\frac{3}{4}x \times 4 = 6 \times 4$

$3x = 24$

Then divide to solve the problem.

$3x \div 3 = 24 \div 3$

$x = 8$

105) The correct answer is B. Substitute 1 for x: $\frac{x-3}{2-x} = \frac{1-3}{2-1} = (1 – 3) \div (2 – 1) = –2 \div 1 = –2$

106) The correct answer is B.
Substitute 5 for the value of x to solve.
$x^2 + xy – y = 41$

$5^2 + 5y - y = 41$
$25 + 5y - y = 41$
$25 - 25 + 5y - y = 41 - 25$
$5y - y = 16$
$4y = 16$
$4y \div 4 = 16 \div 4$
$y = 4$

107) The correct answer is B. Substitute 12 for the value of x. Then simplify and solve.
$x^2 + xy - y = 254$
$12^2 + 12y - y = 254$
$144 + 12y - y = 254$
$144 - 144 + 12y - y = 254 - 144$
$12y - y = 110$
$11y = 110$
$11y \div 11 = 110 \div 11$
$y = 10$

108) The correct answer is C.
$6 + 8(2\sqrt{x} + 4) = 62$
$6 - 6 + 8(2\sqrt{x} + 4) = 62 - 6$
$8(2\sqrt{x} + 4) = 56$
$16\sqrt{x} + 32 = 56$
$16\sqrt{x} + 32 - 32 = 56 - 32$
$16\sqrt{x} = 24$
$16\sqrt{x} \div 16 = 24 \div 16$
$\sqrt{x} = 24 \div 16$
$\sqrt{x} = \dfrac{24}{16}$
$\sqrt{x} = \dfrac{24 \div 8}{16 \div 8} = \dfrac{3}{2}$

109) The correct answer is D. The factors of 50 are: 1 × 50 = 50; 2 × 25 = 50; 5 × 10 = 50. If any of your factors are perfect squares, you can simplify the radical. 25 is a perfect square, so, you need to factor inside the radical sign as shown to solve the problem: $\sqrt{50} = \sqrt{25 \times 2} = \sqrt{5^2 \times 2} = \sqrt{5^2} \times \sqrt{2} = 5\sqrt{2}$

110) The correct answer is D. 36 is the common factor, So, factor the amounts inside the radicals and simplify:
$\sqrt{36} + 4\sqrt{72} - 2\sqrt{144} =$
$\sqrt{36} + 4\sqrt{36 \times 2} - 2\sqrt{36 \times 4} =$
$\sqrt{6 \times 6} + 4\sqrt{(6 \times 6) \times 2} - 2\sqrt{(6 \times 6) \times 4} =$
$6 + (4 \times 6)\sqrt{2} - (2 \times 6)\sqrt{4} =$
$6 + 24\sqrt{2} - (12 \times 2) =$
$6 + 24\sqrt{2} - 24 =$
$-18 + 24\sqrt{2}$

111) The correct answer is A. $\sqrt{7} \times \sqrt{11} = \sqrt{7 \times 11} = \sqrt{77}$

112) The correct answer is B. Add the numbers in front of the radical signs to solve. If there is no number before the radical, then put in the number 1 because then the radical will count only 1 time when you add. $\sqrt{15} + 3\sqrt{15} = 1\sqrt{15} + 3\sqrt{15} = (1 + 3)\sqrt{15} = 4\sqrt{15}$

113) The correct answer is B. The cube root is the number which satisfies the equation when multiplied by itself two times: $\sqrt[3]{\frac{216}{27}} = \sqrt[3]{\frac{6 \times 6 \times 6}{3 \times 3 \times 3}} = \frac{6}{3} = 2$

114) The correct answer is A. The base number is 7. Add the exponents: $7^5 \times 7^3 = 7^{(5+3)} = 7^8$

115) The correct answer is B. The base is xy. Subtract the exponents: $xy^6 \div xy^3 = xy^{(6-3)} = xy^3$

116) The correct answer is C. Perform the operation on the radicals and then simplify.
$\sqrt{8x^4} \cdot \sqrt{32x^6} = \sqrt{8x^4 \times 32x^6} = \sqrt{256x^{10}} = \sqrt{16 \times 16 \times x^5 \times x^5} = 16x^5$

117) The correct answer is B. We have the base number of 10 and we are multiplying, so we can add the exponent of 5 to the exponent of −1: (1.7 × 10⁵ miles per hour) × (2 × 10⁻¹ hours) = 1.7 × 2 × 10$^{(5 + -1)}$ = 3.4 × 10⁴ = 3.4 × 10,000 = 34,000 miles

118) The correct answer is D. When you have a fraction as an exponent, the numerator is new exponent and the denominator goes in front as the root: $\sqrt{x^{\frac{5}{7}}} = \left(\sqrt[7]{x}\right)^5$

119) The correct answer is B. The principle is that $x^{-b} = \frac{1}{x^b}$. Accordingly, $x^{-5} = \frac{1}{x^5}$

120) The correct answer is B. Following the principle mentioned in the answer to question 119, $(-4)^{-3} = \frac{1}{-4^3} = -\frac{1}{64}$

121) The correct answer is C. Any non-zero number raised to the power of zero is equal to 1.

122) The correct answer is C. Any non-zero number multiplied by a variable and raised to the power of zero is equal to 1.

123) The correct answer is C.
$\frac{b + \frac{2}{7}}{\frac{1}{b}} = \left(b + \frac{2}{7}\right) \div \frac{1}{b} = \left(b + \frac{2}{7}\right) \times \frac{b}{1} = b\left(b + \frac{2}{7}\right) = b^2 + \frac{2b}{7}$

124) The correct answer is D. Find the lowest common denominator for the second fraction. Then add the numerators.
$\frac{x^2}{x^2 + 2x} + \frac{8}{x} = \frac{x^2}{x^2 + 2x} + \left(\frac{8}{x} \times \frac{x+2}{x+2}\right) = \frac{x^2}{x^2 + 2x} + \frac{8x + 16}{x^2 + 2x} = \frac{x^2 + 8x + 16}{x^2 + 2x}$

125) The correct answer is A. Multiply as shown: $\dfrac{2a^3}{7} \times \dfrac{3}{a^2} = \dfrac{2a^3 \times 3}{7 \times a^2} = \dfrac{6a^3}{7a^2}$

Then find the greatest common factor and cancel out to simplify: $\dfrac{6a^3}{7a^2} = \dfrac{6a \times a^2}{7 \times a^2} = \dfrac{6a \times \cancel{a^2}}{7 \times \cancel{a^2}} = \dfrac{6a}{7}$

126) The correct answer is B. Invert and multiply.

$\dfrac{8x+8}{x^4} \div \dfrac{5x+5}{x^2} = \dfrac{8x+8}{x^4} \times \dfrac{x^2}{5x+5} = \dfrac{(8x \times x^2) + (8 \times x^2)}{(x^4 \times 5x) + (x^4 \times 5)} = \dfrac{8x^3 + 8x^2}{5x^5 + 5x^4}$

Then factor out $(x+1)$ from the numerator and denominator and cancel out:

$\dfrac{8x^3 + 8x^2}{5x^5 + 5x^4} = \dfrac{(8x^2 \times x) + (8x^2 \times 1)}{(5x^4 \times x) + (5x^4 \times 1)} = \dfrac{8x^2(x+1)}{5x^4(x+1)} = \dfrac{8x^2\cancel{(x+1)}}{5x^4\cancel{(x+1)}} = \dfrac{8x^2}{5x^4}$

Finally, factor out x^2 and cancel it out: $\dfrac{8x^2}{5x^4} = \dfrac{x^2 \times 8}{x^2 \times 5x^2} = \dfrac{\cancel{x^2} \times 8}{\cancel{x^2} \times 5x^2} = \dfrac{8}{5x^2}$

127) The correct answer is A. The factors of 9 are: 1 × 9 = 9; **3** × **3** = 9. The factors of 3 are: 1 × **3** = 3. So, put the integer for the common factor outside the parentheses first: $9x^3 - 3x = 3(3x^3 - x)$
Then determine if there are any common variables for the terms that remain in the parentheses. For $(3x^2 - x)$ the terms $3x^2$ and x have the variable x in common. So, now factor out x to solve:
$3(3x^3 - x) = 3x(3x^2 - 1)$

128) The correct answer is B. Looking at this expression, we can see that each term contains x. We can also see that each term contains y. So, first factor out xy: $2xy - 6x^2y + 4x^2y^2 = xy(2 - 6x + 4xy)$. We can also see that all of the terms inside the parentheses are divisible by 2. Now let's factor out the 2. To do this, we divide each term inside the parentheses by 2: $xy(2 - 6x + 4xy) = 2xy(1 - 3x + 2xy)$

129) The correct answer is C. The line in a fraction is the same as the division symbol. For example, $a/b = a \div b$. In the same way, $3/xy = 3 \div (xy)$.

130) The correct answer is A. You should use the FOIL method in this problem. Be very careful with the negative numbers when doing the multiplication.
$2(x+2)(x-3) =$
$2[(x \times x) + (x \times -3) + (2 \times x) + (2 \times -3)] =$
$2(x^2 + -3x + 2x + -6) =$
$2(x^2 - 3x + 2x - 6) =$
$2(x^2 - x - 6)$

Then multiply each term by the 2 at the front of the parentheses.
$2(x^2 - x - 6) =$
$2x^2 - 2x - 12$

131) The correct answer is A. To divide, invert the second fraction and then multiply as shown.
$\dfrac{x}{5} \div \dfrac{9}{y} = \dfrac{x}{5} \times \dfrac{y}{9} = \dfrac{x \times y}{5 \times 9} = \dfrac{xy}{45}$

132) The correct answer is D. Use the FOIL method to expand the polynomial.
FIRST – Multiply the first term from the first set of parentheses by the first term from the second set of parentheses: **(x + 4y)**(**x** + 4y) = x × x = x²
OUTSIDE – Multiply the first term from the first set of parentheses by the second term from the second set of parentheses: (**x** + 4y)(x + **4y**) = x × 4y = 4xy
INSIDE – Multiply the second term from the first set of parentheses by the first term from the second set of parentheses: (x + **4y**)(**x** + 4y) = 4y × x = 4xy
LAST– Multiply the second term from the first set of parentheses by the second term from the second set of parentheses: (x + **4y**)(x + **4y**) = 4y × 4y = 16y²
Finally, we add all of the products together: x² + 4xy + 4xy + 16y² = x² + 8xy + 16y²

133) The correct answer is D. $(2 + \sqrt{6})^2 = (2 + \sqrt{6})(2 + \sqrt{6}) =$
$(2 \times 2) + (2 \times \sqrt{6}) + (2 \times \sqrt{6}) + (\sqrt{6} \times \sqrt{6}) = 4 + 4\sqrt{6} + 6 = 10 + 4\sqrt{6}$

134) The correct answer is C. As the quantity of sugar increases, the amount of sleep also increases. A positive linear relationship therefore exists between the two variables. This is represented in chart C since the amount of sleep is greater when the amount of sugar consumed is higher.

135) The correct answer is C. We can see that the line does not begin on exactly on (5, 5), nor does it begin on (5, 9) because the first point is slightly below the horizontal line for y = 5. Therefore, we can rule out answers A and D. If we look at x = 20 on the graph, we can see that y = 18 at this point. We can express this as the function: $f(x) = x \times 0.9$. Putting in the values of x from chart (C), we get the following: 5 × 0.9 = 4.5; 10 × 0.9 = 9; 15 × 0.9 =13.5; 20 × 0.9 = 18. This is represented in table C.

136) The correct answer is C. Put the value provided for x into the function to solve. $f_1(2) = 5^2 = 25$

137) The correct answer is D. First, solve for the function in the inner-most set of parentheses, in this case $f_1(x)$. To solve, you simply have to look at the first table. Find the value of 2 in the first column and the related value in the second column. For x = 2, $f_1(2)$ = 5. Then, take this new value to solve for $f_2(x)$. Look at the second table. Find the value of 5 in the first column and the related value in the second column. For x = 5, $f_2(5)$ = 25.

138) The correct answer is C. Two whole numbers that are greater than 1 will always result in a greater number when they are multiplied by each other, rather than when those numbers are divided by each other or subtracted from each other. So, for positive integers, x × y will always be greater than the following:
x ÷ y
y ÷ x
x – y
y – x
1 ÷ x
1 ÷ y

139) The correct answer is B. Substitute x + 3 for x in the original function to solve. So, $x^2 + 3x - 8$ becomes $(x + 3)^2 + 3(x + 3) - 8$

140) The correct answer is B. First, you need to convert the logarithmic function into an exponential equation. To convert a logarithmic function to an exponent, the number after the equals sign (4 in this problem) becomes the exponent. The small subscript number after "log" (3 in this problem) becomes the base number. So, the exponential equation for $\log_3(x + 2) = 4$ is $3^4 = x + 2$. Then find the result for the exponent: $3^4 = 3 \times 3 \times 3 \times 3 = 81$. Substituting 81 on the left side of the equation, we get $81 = x + 2$. Therefore, $x = 79$.

141) The correct answer is D. If a term or variable is subtracted within the parentheses, you have to keep the negative sign with it when you multiply.
FIRST: $(\mathbf{x} - y)(\mathbf{x} + y) = x \times x = x^2$
OUTSIDE: $(\mathbf{x} - y)(x + \mathbf{y}) = x \times y = xy$
INSIDE: $(x - \mathbf{y})(\mathbf{x} + y) = -y \times x = -xy$
LAST: $(x - \mathbf{y})(x + \mathbf{y}) = -y \times y = -y^2$
SOLUTION: $x^2 + xy + - xy - y^2 = x^2 - y^2$

142) The correct answer is A.
FIRST: $(\mathbf{3x} + y)(\mathbf{x} - 5y) = 3x \times x = 3x^2$
OUTSIDE: $(\mathbf{3x} + y)(x - \mathbf{5y}) = 3x \times -5y = -15xy$
INSIDE: $(3x + \mathbf{y})(\mathbf{x} - 5y) = y \times x = xy$
LAST: $(3x + \mathbf{y})(x - \mathbf{5y}) = y \times -5y = -5y^2$
Then add all of the above once you have completed FOIL: $3x^2 - 15xy + xy - 5y^2 = 3x^2 - 14xy - 5y^2$

143) The correct answer is A. First, Isolate the whole numbers.
$50 - \frac{3x}{5} \geq 41$
$(50 - 50) - \frac{3x}{5} \geq 41 - 50$
$-\frac{3x}{5} \geq -9$
Then get rid of the denominator on the fraction.
$-\frac{3x}{5} \geq -9$
$\left(5 \times -\frac{3x}{5}\right) \geq -9 \times 5$
$-3x \geq -9 \times 5$
$-3x \geq -45$
Then isolate the remaining whole numbers.
$-3x \geq -45$
$-3x \div 3 \geq -45 \div 3$
$-x \geq -45 \div 3$
$-x \geq -15$
Then deal with the negative number.
$-x \geq -15$
$-x + 15 \geq -15 + 15$
$-x + 15 \geq 0$
Finally, isolate the unknown variable as a positive number.
$-x + 15 \geq 0$
$-x + x + 15 \geq 0 + x$

$15 \geq x$
$x \leq 15$

144) The correct answer is D. Substitute 5 for $x - 2$ as shown: $x - 2 > 5$ and $x - 2 = y$, so $y > 5$. If two wizfits are being purchased, we need to solve for $2y$:
$y \times 2 > 5 \times 2$
$2y > 10$

145) The correct answer is B. For quadratic inequality problems like this one, you need to factor the inequality first. The factors of -9 are: -1×9; -3×3; 1×-9. Because we do not have a term with only the x variable, we need factors that add up to zero, so factor as shown:
$x^2 - 9 < 0$
$(x + 3)(x - 3) < 0$
Then find values for x by solving each parenthetical for 0.
$(x + 3) = 0$
$(-3 + 3) = 0$
$x = -3$
$(x - 3) = 0$
$(3 - 3) = 0$
$x = 3$
So, $x > -3$ or $x < 3$

You can then check your work to be sure that you have the inequality signs pointing the right way.
Use -2 to check $x > -3$. Since $-2 > -3$ is correct, our proof should also be correct:
$x^2 - 9 < 0$
$-2^2 - 9 < 0$
$4 - 9 < 0$
$-5 < 0$ CORRECT

Use 4 to check for $x < 3$. Since $4 < 3$ is incorrect, our proof should also be incorrect.
$x^2 - 9 < 0$
$4^2 - 9 < 0$
$16 - 9 < 0$
$7 < 0$ INCORRECT

Therefore, we have checked that $x > -3$ or $x < 3$.

146) The correct answer is B.
Factor: $x^2 - 5x + 6 \leq 0$
$(x - 2)(x - 3) \leq 0$

Then solve each parenthetical for zero:
$(x - 2) = 0$
$2 - 2 = 0$
$x = 2$
$(x - 3) = 0$
$3 - 3 = 0$
$x = 3$

So, $2 \leq x \leq 3$

Now check. Use 1 to check to $2 \leq x$, which is the same as $x \geq 2$. Since 1 is not actually greater than or equal to 2, our proof for this should be incorrect.
$x^2 - 5x + 6 \leq 0$
$1^2 - (5 \times 1) + 6 \leq 0$
$1 - 5 + 6 \leq 0$
$-4 + 6 \leq 0$
$2 \leq 0$ INCORRECT

Use 2.5 to check for $x \leq 3$. Since 2.5 really is less than 3, our proof should be correct.
$x^2 - 5x + 6 \leq 0$
$2.5^2 - (5 \times 2.5) + 6 \leq 0$
$6.25 - 12.5 + 6 \leq 0$
$-0.25 \leq 0$ CORRECT

Therefore, we have checked that $2 \leq x \leq 3$

147) The correct answer is D. We know that the products of 12 are: $1 \times 12 = 12$; $2 \times 6 = 12$; $3 \times 4 = 12$. So, add each of the two factors together to solve the first equation: $1 + 12 = 13$; $2 + 6 = 8$; $3 + 4 = 7$. (3, 4) solves both equations, so it is the correct answer.

148) The correct answer is C. The first term of the second equation is x. To eliminate the x variable, we need to multiply the second equation by 3 because the first equation contains 3x.
$x + 2y = 8$
$(3 \times x) + (3 \times 2y) = (3 \times 8)$
$3x + 6y = 24$
Now subtract the new second equation from the original first equation.
$3x + 3y = 15$
$\underline{-(3x + 6y = 24)}$
$-3y = -9$
Then solve for y.
$-3y = -9$
$-3y \div -3 = -9 \div -3$
$y = 3$

Using our original second equation of $x + 2y = 8$, substitute the value of 3 for y to solve for x.
$x + 2y = 8$
$x + (2 \times 3) = 8$
$x + 6 = 8$
$x + 6 - 6 = 8 - 6$
$x = 2$

149) The correct answer is B. There is a difference of 4 between each number in the sequence. Where variable *a* represents your starting number and variable *d* represents the difference, you could write an arithmetic sequence like this: a, a + d, a + 2d, a + 3d, a + 4d, a + 5d, . . .
However, it is easier to remember that the formula for the nth number of an arithmetic sequence is:
a + [d × (n − 1)] We can prove that 21 is the sixth number of the sequence in our problem by putting the values into the formula.
a = 1
d = 4
n = 6
a + [d × (n − 1)]
1 + [4 × (6 − 1)] =
1 + (4 × 5) =
1 + 20 = 21

150) The correct answer is D. Each number in the sequence is found by multiplying by a factor of 3:
2 × 3 = 6
6 × 3 = 18
18 × 3 = 54

So, each subsequent number is found by multiplying the previous number by 3. Where the first number is represented by variable *a* and the factor (called the "common ratio") is represented by variable *r*, you could write out a geometric sequence like this: a, ar, a(r)^2, a(r)^3 . . .
The sequence in this problem starts at 2 and triples each time, so a = 2 (the first term) and r = 3 (the "common ratio"). Remember that the formula for calculating the nth item in a geometric sequence is as follows: ar$^{(n-1)}$
So, let's consider our example problem again.
2, 6, 18, 54, . . .
The fifth term of the sequence is 54 × 3 = 162.

We can check this by putting the values into our formula: ar$^{(n-1)}$
a = 2 (the first term)
r = 3 (the "common ratio")
n = 5

2 × 3$^{(5-1)}$ =
2 × 3^4 =
2 × 81 = 162

151) The correct answer is C. The problem states that you get a $59 subscription for every new customer, so we need to multiply the amount of the subscription fee by the number of new customers to solve: $59 × 14 = $826

152) The correct answer is D. Perform the operation as shown: 35 − (−92) = 127. Express your result as a positive number since the value has increased from year 1 to year 2.

153) The correct answer is C. The problem is asking for the total for all three years, so we add the three amounts together: $12,225 + $43,871 + $69,423= $125,519

154) The correct answer is A. Take the amount of money the customer gives the cashier and subtract the amount of the change provided to calculate the amount of the purchase: $75.00 − $8.35 = $66.65

155) The correct answer is C. Add to solve: −205 + 39 − 107 + 18 + 126 = −129

156) The correct answer is C. Step 1 − Determine the total number of hours worked: 7.5 hours per day for 2 days = 7.5 × 2 = 15 hours. Step 2 − Calculate the profit your company makes per hour. The customer was billed $75 per hour for your work, and you were paid $40 per hour: $75 − $40 = $35 profit per hour. Step 3 − Multiply the total number of hours by the profit per hour to solve: 15 hours × $35 profit per hour = $525

157) The correct answer is D. Step 1 − Add the whole numbers: 4 + 3 = 7. Step 2 − Add the fractions: 3/8 + 7/8 = 10/8. Step 3 − Simplify the fraction from Step 2: 10/8 = 8/8 + 2/8 = 1 + 2/8 = $1^{2}/_{8}$ = $1^{1}/_{4}$. Step 4 − Combine the results from Step 1 and Step 3 to solve the problem: 7 + $1^{1}/_{4}$ = $8^{1}/_{4}$

158) The correct answer is C. In this problem, the fraction on the second number is larger than the fraction on the first number, so we need to convert the first fraction before we start our calculation. Step 1 − Convert $12^{7}/_{16}$ for subtraction: $12^{7}/_{16}$ = $11^{7}/_{16}$ + 1 = $11^{7}/_{16}$ + $^{16}/_{16}$ = $11^{23}/_{16}$. Step 2 − There were $8^{9}/_{16}$ yards left, so subtract the whole numbers: 11 − 8 = 3. Step 3 − Subtract the fractions: 23/16 − 9/16 = 14/16. Step 4 − Simplify the fraction from Step 3: 14/16 = (14 ÷ 2)/(16 ÷ 2) = 7/8. Step 4 − Combine the results from Step 2 and Step 4 to get your new mixed number to solve the problem: 3 + 7/8 = $3^{7}/_{8}$

159) The correct answer is B. The problem tells us the relative amount of units sold, but the question is asking for the relative amount of units left. So, subtract the decimal from 1 to find the relative amount left: 1 − 0.75 = 0.25. Then multiply the total number of items at the start by this decimal number: 80 items × 0.25 = 80 × 0.25 = 20 items left

160) The correct answer is B. In our problem, if t% subscribe to digital TV packages, then 100% − t% do not subscribe. In other words, since a percentage is any given number out of 100%, the percentage of students who do not subscribe is represented by this equation: (100% − t%). This equation is then multiplied by the total number of students (n) in order to determine the number of students who do not subscribe to digital TV packages: (100% − t%) × n

161) The correct answer is C. Step 1 − Set up the original proportion as a fraction. We have 3 parts of icing sugar for every 6 parts of sugar paste so our fraction is $^{3}/_{6}$. Step 2 − You can simplify the fraction from the previous step because both the numerator and denominator are divisible by 3: $^{3}/_{6}$ ÷ $^{3}/_{3}$ = $^{1}/_{2}$. Step 3 − We need to use 14 parts of sugar paste for the current batch, so multiply this amount by the simplified fraction. $^{1}/_{2}$ × 14 = 7

162) The correct answer is A. This problem is asking for the ratio of non-faulty mp3 players to the quantity of faulty mp3 players. Therefore, you must put the quantity of non-faulty mp3 players before the colon in the ratio. In this problem, 1% of the players are faulty. 1% × 100 = 1 faulty player in every 100 players. 100 − 1 = 99 non-faulty players. So, the ratio is 99:1. The number before the colon and the number after the colon can be added together to get the total quantity.

163) The correct answer is B. The sales price of each cell phone is four times the cost. The cost is expressed as x, so the sales price is $4x$. The difference between the sales price of each cell phone and the cost of each cell phone is the profit. In this problem, the sales price is $4x$ and the cost is x.
Sales Price − Cost = Profit
$4x - x$ = Profit
$3x$ = Profit

164) The correct answer is D. The price of the internet connection is always 5 times the speed.
$10 = 2 \times 5$
$20 = 4 \times 5$
$30 = 6 \times 5$
$40 = 8 \times 5$
So, the price of the internet connection (represented by variable P) equals the speed (represented by variable s) times 5: $P = s \times 5$

165) The correct answer is C. To calculate the mean, add up all of the values: $1 + 2 + 3 + 4 + 5 + 5 + 8 + 8 + 9 = 45$. There are 9 numbers in the set, so we need to divide by 9: $45 \div 9 = 5$

166) The correct answer is C. To find the median, first you have to put the numbers in the data set in the correct order from lowest to highest: 3, 12, 18, **20**, 25, 28, 30. The median is the middle number in the set, which is 20 in this question.

167) The correct answer is C. In order to solve the problem, take the second equation and isolate J on one side of the equation. By doing this, you define variable J in terms of variable T.
$J + 2T = \$40$
$J + 2T - 2T = \$40 - 2T$
$J = \$40 - 2T$

Now substitute $\$40 - 2T$ for variable J in the first equation to solve for variable T.
$2J + T = 50$
$2(40 - 2T) + T = 50$
$80 - 4T + T = 50$
$80 - 3T = 50$
$80 - 3T + 3T = 50 + 3T$
$80 = 50 + 3T$
$80 - 50 = 50 - 50 + 3T$
$30 = 3T$
$30 \div 3 = 3T \div 3$
$10 = T$

So, now that we know that a T-shirt costs $10, we can substitute this value in one of the equations in order to find the value for the jeans, which is variable J.
$2J + T = 50$
$2J + 10 = 50$
$2J + 10 - 10 = 50 - 10$
$2J = 40$
$2J \div 2 = 40 \div 2$
$J = 20$
Now solve for the customer's purchase. If the customer purchased one pair of jeans and one T-shirt, then she paid: $10 + $20 = $30

168) The correct answer is B. Step 1 – Subtract one increment: $23/64 - 1/64 = 22/64$. Step 2 – Simplify your result: $22/64 = (22 \div 2)/(64 \div 2) = 11/32$

169) The correct answer is B. Step 1 – Work out the cost for the usual supplier: 325 pairs × $4 = $1,300. Step 2 – Calculate the price for the second supplier: $1,250 + ($1,250 × .06) = $1,250 + $75 = $1,325. Step 3 – Compare to the third deal to solve: The third deal is $1,290 so this is the best deal.

170) The correct answer is C. We have a formula to convert meters to centimeters and another formula to convert inches to centimeters, so we will need to use those two formulas to solve the problem. Step 1 – Determine the measurement in centimeters: 1 meter = 100 centimeters. Step 2 – Convert the centimeters to inches. The formulas states that 1 inch = 2.54 centimeters. However, we need to use the formula in reverse because we are converting centimeters to inches. So, divide to solve: 100 ÷ 2.54 = 39.37 inches

171) The correct answer is C. The sum of all three angles inside a triangle is always 180 degrees. So, we need to deduct the degrees given from 180° to find out the total degrees of the two other angles: 180° − 36° = 144°. Now divide this result by two in order to determine the degrees for each angle: 144° ÷ 2 = 72°

172) The correct answer is A. The area of a rectangle is equal to its length times its width. This football field is 30 yards wide and 100 yards long, so we can substitute the values into the appropriate formula.
rectangle area = width × length
rectangle area = 30 × 100
rectangle area = 3000

173) The correct answer is B. You are being asked about the distance around the outside, so you need to calculate the per meter, Write out the formula: (length × 2) + (width × 2). Then substitute the values: (5 × 2) + (3 × 2) = 10 + 6 = 16

174) The correct answer is B. Substitute the value of the diameter into the formula to solve.
circumference ≈ diameter × 3.14
circumference ≈ 12 × 3.14

175) The correct answer is D. To calculate the volume of a box, you need the formula for a rectangular solid: volume = base × width × height. Now substitute the values from the problem into the formula.
volume = 20 × 15 × 25 = 7500

176) The correct answer is C. Step 1 – Determine the amount of seconds that have passed from 6:00 AM to 6:10 AM. 10 minutes × 60 seconds per minute = 600 seconds production time. Step 2 – Subtract the packaging time. 600 seconds − 5 seconds packaging per box = 595 seconds available for production. Step 3 – Determine the production time per unit: (9 seconds production time + 2 seconds set-up time) × 6 stages = 11 seconds × 6 = 66 seconds per unit. Step 4 – Divide the available production time by the time per unit to determine how many items can be produced. 595 seconds ÷ 66 seconds = 9.015 units, which we round down to 9.

177) The correct answer is B. Step 1 – Find the total product weight, excluding the weight of the crate. 447 pounds − 60 pounds = 387 pounds. Step 2 – Convert the total product weight to ounces. 387 pounds × 16 ounces per pound = 6,192 ounces of total product weight. Step 3 – Convert the weight of each unit to ounces: 32 pounds and 4 ounces = (32 × 16) + 4 = 512 + 4 = 516 ounces each. Step 4 – Divide to solve: 6,192 ÷ 516 = 12 units

178) The correct answer is C. Step 1 – Determine the actual distance between the two cities in miles. 1 inch on the map = 20 miles, so 2.5 inches × 20 = 50 miles actual distance. Step 2 – Convert the result from Step 1 to kilometers. 1 mile = 1.61 kilometers, so 50 miles × 1.61 = 80.5 kilometers.

179) The correct answer is C. Step 1 – Determine the rate for the packaging: 1.5 hours ÷ 5 boxes = 90 minutes ÷ 5 boxes = 18 minutes per box. Step 2 – Add 4 extra minutes per box to the rate to account for the time to fill in the shipping form. 18 + 4 = 22 minutes per box needed in total. Step 3 – Calculate the time needed to package all 14 boxes and prepare them for shipment: 22 minutes × 14 = 308 minutes = 5 hours and 8 minutes

180) The correct answer is A. Step 1 – Calculate the amount of ounces needed to fill the small bottles: 25 bottles × 8 ounces each = 200 ounces. Step 2 – Calculate the amount of ounces needed to fill the large bottles: 20 bottles × 12 ounces each = 240 ounces. Step 3 – Add the ounces needed for the bottles and convert to quarts. There are 8 ounces in a cup, and there are 4 cups in a quart, so there are 32 ounces in a quart: 200 ounces + 240 ounces = 440 ounces ÷ 32 ounces in a quart = 13.75 quarts, which we round up to 14 quarts. Step 4 – Add the amount needed for the bottles to the amount required for stock: 14 quarts + 4 quarts = 18 quarts. Step 5 – Subtract the beginning stock from the total amount needed: 18 – 3 = 15 more quarts needed. The treatment is sold in 2 quart containers, so our result needs to be a multiple of 2, so we round up to 16 quarts, which equals 8 containers.

181) The correct answer is A. If no number is duplicated, then we say that the data set has no mode.

182) The correct answer is A. The outcome of an earlier roll does not affect the outcome of the next roll. When rolling a pair of dice, the possibility of an odd number is always $1/2$, just as the possibility of an even number is always $1/2$. We can prove this mathematically by looking at the possible outcomes:
1,1 1,2 1,3 1,4 1,5 1,6
2,1 2,2 2,3 2,4 2,5 2,6
3,1 3,2 3,3 3,4 3,5 3,6
4,1 4,2 4,3 4,4 4,5 4,6
5,1 5,2 5,3 5,4 5,5 5,6
6,1 6,2 6,3 6,4 6,5 6,6
The odd number combinations are highlighted:
1,1 **1,2** 1,3 **1,4** 1,5 **1,6**
2,1 2,2 **2,3** 2,4 **2,5** 2,6
3,1 **3,2** 3,3 **3,4** 3,5 **3,6**
4,1 4,2 **4,3** 4,4 **4,5** 4,6
5,1 **5,2** 5,3 **5,4** 5,5 **5,6**
6,1 6,2 **6,3** 6,4 **6,5** 6,6
So, we can see that an odd number will be rolled half of the time.

183) The correct answer is B. Bookcase A is 8 feet long and 2 feet deep, so multiply to solve:
8 × 2 = 16 square feet

184) The correct answer B. is Bookcase B is 5 feet long and two feet deep: 5 × 2 = 10 square feet

185) The correct answer is C. The area of the entire room is calculated as follows: 8 feet × 12 feet = 96 square feet. However, flooring is not placed under the bookcases, so subtract the square footage under the bookcases, which we calculated in the two previous questions, to solve: 96 – 16 – 10 = 70 square feet. Each piece of flooring is 1 square foot, so 70 pieces of flooring are needed.

186) The correct answer is B. 70 square feet × $5.50 per piece = $385 total cost

187) The correct answer is C. Subtract the percentage of the discount from 100% to get the percentage of the price to be paid: 100% - 27.5% = 72.5%. Multiply to solve: $385 × 72.5% = $279.13, which is closest to $280.

188) The correct answer is D. The total number of patients is 793,000 and 89% of them have survived, so multiply to solve: 793,000 × 0.89 = 705,770

189) The correct answer is. C. This is a more complicated question. You need to determine the death rate, so subtract the survival rate from 100% to get the death rate for each category. Then multiply for each category and compare:
Cardiopulmonary and vascular deaths: 602,000 × 0.18 = 108,360
HIV/AIDS deaths: 215,000 × 0.27 = 58,050
Diabetes deaths: 793,000 × 0.11 = 87,230
Cancer and leukemia deaths: 231,000 × 0.52 =120,120
Deaths from premature birth complications: 68,000 × 0.36 = 24,480
So cancer and leukemia caused the greatest number of deaths.

190) The correct answer is C. Cancer and leukemia deaths: 231,000 × 0.52 = 120,120, which is closest to 120,000.

191) The correct answer is A. Refer to your calculations for question 189 and add the two smallest amounts together: 24,480 + 58,050 = 82,530

192) The correct answer is B. We know from the second equation that y is equal to $x + 7$. So put $x + 7$ into the first equation for the value of y to solve.
$-3x - 1 = y$
$-3x - 1 = x + 7$
$-3x - 1 + 1 = x + 7 + 1$
$-3x - x = x - x + 8$
$-4x = 8$
$-4x \div -4 = 8 \div -4$
$x = -2$
Now we know that the value of x is –2, so we can put that into the equation to solve for y.
$-3x - 1 = y$
$(-3 \times -2) - 1 = y$
$6 - 1 = y$
$y = 5$

193) The correct answer is D. To answer this type of question, you need these principles: (a) Positive numbers are greater than negative numbers; (b) When two fractions have the same numerator, the fraction with the smaller number in the denominator is the larger fraction. Accordingly, 1 is greater than $1/5$; $1/5$ is greater than $1/7$, and $1/7$ is greater than $-1/3$.

194) The correct answer is C. Add 9 to each side to get rid of the integer on the left.
$3x - 9 = -18$
$3x - 9 + 9 = -18 + 9$
$3x = -9$
Then divide each side by 3 to solve.
$3x \div 3 = -9 \div 3$
$x = -3$

195) The correct answer is A. Substitute 7 for x to solve.
$2x^2 + 8x =$
$[2(7)^2] + (8 \times 7) =$
$(2 \times 49) + 56 =$
$98 + 56 = 154$

196) The correct answer is D. Put the values provided for x into the function to solve.
$f_1 = x^2 + x = 5^2 + 5 = 25 + 5 = 30$

197) The correct answer is B. $4^{11} \times 4^8 = 4^{(11 + 8)} = 4^{19}$

198) The correct answer is A. Expand by multiplying the terms as shown below:
FIRST: $(\mathbf{x} - 5)(\mathbf{3x} + 8) = x \times 3x = 3x^2$
OUTSIDE: $(\mathbf{x} - 5)(3x + \mathbf{8}) = x \times 8 = 8x$
INSIDE: $(x - \mathbf{5})(\mathbf{3x} + 8) = -5 \times 3x = -15x$
LAST: $(x - \mathbf{5})(3x + \mathbf{8}) = -5 \times 8 = -40$
Then add all of the individual results together: $3x^2 + 8x + -15x + -40 = 3x^2 - 7x - 40$

199) The correct answer is C. In order to find the value of a variable inside a square root sign, you need to square each side of the equation.
$\sqrt{9z + 18} = 9$
$\sqrt{9z + 18}^2 = 9^2$
$9z + 18 = 81$
$9z + 18 - 18 = 81 - 18$
$9z = 63$
$9z \div 9 = 63 \div 9$
$z = 7$

200) The correct answer is C. First you need to get rid of the fraction. To eliminate the fraction, multiply each side of the equation by the denominator of the fraction.
$z = \dfrac{x}{1 - y}$
$z \times (1 - y) = \dfrac{x}{1 - y} \times (1 - y)$
$z(1 - y) = x$

Then isolate y to solve.
$z(1 - y) \div z = x \div z$
$1 - y = x \div z$
$1 - 1 - y = (x \div z) - 1$
$-y = (x \div z) - 1$
$-y \times -1 = [(x \div z) - 1] \times -1$
$y = -\dfrac{x}{z} + 1$

TABE 9 & 10 Practice Test 2 – Solutions and Explanations

201) The correct answer is B. Divide the total amount by the sales price per unit to solve: $7,375 ÷ $59 = 125 units sold

202) The correct answer is D. Add the growth and subtract the decreases: 52 – 14 + 37 – 28 + 61 = 108

203) The correct answer is C. Divide and then express the result as a percentage. Step 1 – Treat the line in the fraction as the division symbol: 6/25 = 6 ÷ 25 = 0.24. Step 2 – To express the result from Step 1 as a percentage, move the decimal point two places to the right and add the percent sign: 0.24 = 24.0%

204) The correct answer is C. Move the decimal point two places to the right and add the percent sign: 0.40 = 40.0%

205) The correct answer is D. First of all, you need to determine the difference in temperature during the entire time period: 62 – 38 = 24 degrees less. Then calculate how much time has passed. From 5:00 PM to 11:00 PM, 6 hours have passed. Next, divide the temperature difference by the amount of time that has passed to get the temperature change per hour: 24 degrees ÷ 6 hours = 4 degrees less per hour. To calculate the temperature at the stated time, you need to calculate the time difference. From 5:00 PM to 9:00 PM, 4 hours have passed. So, the temperature difference during the stated time is 4 hours × 4 degrees per hour = 16 degrees less. Finally, deduct this from the beginning temperature to get your final answer: 62°F – 16°F = 46°F

206) The correct answer is C. The number of hot dogs is D and the number of hamburgers is H. The equation to express the problem is: $(D × \$2.50) + (H × \$4) = \$22$. We know that the number of hamburgers is 3, so put that in the equation and solve it.
$(D × \$2.50) + (H × \$4) = \$22$
$(D × \$2.50) + (3 × \$4) = \$22$
$(D × \$2.50) + 12 = \$22$
$(D × \$2.50) + 12 – 12 = \$22 – 12$
$(D × \$2.50) = \$10$
$\$2.50D = \$10$
$\$2.50D ÷ \$2.50 = \$10 ÷ \$2.50$
$D = 4$

207) The correct answer is C. For your first step, determine how many square feet there are in total: 2000 square feet per room × 8 rooms = 16,000 square feet in total. Then you need to divide by the coverage rate: 16,000 square feet to cover ÷ 900 square feet coverage per bucket = 17.77 buckets needed. It is not possible to purchase a partial bucket of paint, so 17.77 is rounded up to 18 buckets of paint.

208) The correct answer is A. Divide the distance traveled by the time in order to get the speed in miles per hour. Remember that in order to divide by a fraction, you need to invert the fraction, and then multiply.
3.6 miles ÷ ³/₄ =
3.6 × ⁴/₃ =
(3.6 × 4) ÷ 3 =
14.4 ÷ 3 = 4.8 miles per hour

209) The correct answer is C. Step 1 – Determine the dollar amount of the reduction or discount: $60 original price – $45 sale price = $15 discount. Step 2 – Then divide the discount by the original price to get the percentage of the discount: $15 ÷ $60 = 0.25 = 25%

210) The correct answer is B. For your first step, add the subsets of the ratio together: 6 + 7 = 13. Then divide this into the total: 117 ÷ 13 = 9. Finally, multiply the result from the previous step by the subset of males from the original ratio: 6 × 9 = 54 males in the class

211) The correct answer is B. First add up all of the values: 1 + 1 + 3 + 2 + 4 + 3 + 1 + 2 + 1 = 18 There are nine values, so we divide to get the mean: 18 ÷ 9 = 2

212) The correct answer is D. Set up your equation to calculate the average, using x for the age of the 5th sibling:
$(2 + 5 + 7 + 12 + x) \div 5 = 8$
$(2 + 5 + 7 + 12 + x) \div 5 \times 5 = 8 \times 5$
$(2 + 5 + 7 + 12 + x) = 40$
$26 + x = 40$
$26 - 26 + x = 40 - 26$
$x = 14$

213) The correct answer is B. The problem provides the number set: 8.19, 7.59, 8.25, 7.35, 9.10. First of all, put the numbers in ascending order: 7.35, 7.59, 8.19, 8.25, 9.10. Then find the one that is in the middle: 7.35, 7.59, **8.19**, 8.25, 9.10

214) The correct answer is C. For 2 sandwiches, the total price is $17.50, so each sandwich in this deal sells for $8.75: $17.50 total price ÷ 2 sandwiches = $8.75 each. For 4 sandwiches, the total price is $34.40, so each sandwich in this deal sells for $8.60: $34.40 total price ÷ 4 sandwiches = $8.60 each. For 8 sandwiches, the total price is $68, so each sandwich in this deal sells for $8.50: $68 total price ÷ 8 sandwiches = $8.50 each. So, the best price per sandwich is $8.50.

215) The correct answer is B. First, determine the total sales value of the cheese and pepperoni pizzas based on the prices stated in the problem: (15 cheese pizzas × $10 each) + (10 pepperoni pizzas × $12 each) = $150 + $120 = $270. The remaining amount is allocable to the vegetable pizzas: Total sales of $310 − $270 = $40 worth of vegetable pizzas. The problems states that 5 vegetable pizzas were sold. We calculate the price of the vegetable pizzas as follows: $40 worth of vegetable pizzas ÷ 5 vegetable pizzas sold = $8 per vegetable pizza

216) The correct answer is C. Shanika wants to earn $4,000 this month. She gets the $1,000 basic pay regardless of the number of cars she sells, so we need to subtract that from the total first: $4,000 − $1,000 = $3,000. She gets $390 for each car she sells, so we need to divide that into the remaining $3,000: $3,000 to earn ÷ $390 per car = 7.69 cars to sell. Since it is not possible to sell a part of a car, we need to round up to 8 cars.

217) The correct answer is D. First, we can perform division to determine that the plane travels 6.5 miles per minute: 780 miles ÷ 120 minutes = 6.5 miles per minute. Since the plane travels at a constant speed, we multiply this amount by 40 minutes to solve: 6.5 miles per minute × 40 minutes = 260 miles

218) The correct answer is D. Step 1 – Determine the amount of time in seconds: 2 minutes and 48 seconds = (2 minutes × 60 seconds per minute) + 48 seconds = 120 seconds + 48 seconds = 168 seconds. Step 2 – Divide by the amount of furlongs to find the rate: 168 seconds ÷ 12 furlongs = 14 seconds per furlong

219) The correct answer is C. Step 1 – Take the total number of viewers and divide this by the 100 viewers in the original ratio: 3200 ÷ 100 = 32. Step 2 – Take the result from Step 1 and multiply by the amount in the subset to solve: 32 × 30 = 960

220) The correct answer is A. Step 1 – Add the charge for postage and handling to the original price per item: $22 + $ 3 = $25. Step 2 – Take the result from Step 1 and multiply by the number of items sold: $25 × 32 = $800

221) The correct answer is B. Step 1 – Add the whole numbers: 107 + 96 = 203. Step 2 – Add the fractions: 3/8 + 1/8 = 4/8 = 1/2. Step 3 – Combine the results from Step 1 and Step 2 to get your new mixed number to solve the problem: 203 + 1/2 = 203$\frac{1}{2}$

222) The correct answer is C. Add the four figures together to solve: 163.75 + 107.50 + 91.25 + 10.30 = 372.80

223) The correct answer is B. Step 1 – Find the amount of material needed for each quilt: 2 yards red, 4 yards blue, 1.2 yards gold (6 ÷ 5 = 1.2), and 0.5 yards white = 2 + 4 + 1.2 + 0.5 = 7.7 yards each. Step 2 – Multiply the total number of quilts by the amount of yards per quilt to solve: 10 × 7.7 = 77

224) The correct answer is C. Each panel is 8 feet 6 inches long, and you need 11 panels to cover the entire side of the field. So, we need to multiply 8 feet 6 inches by 11. Step 1 – 8 feet × 11 = 88 feet. Step 2 – 6 inches × 11 = 66 inches. Step 3 – Now simplify the result. There are 12 inches in a foot, so we need to determine how many feet and inches there are in 66 inches. 66 inches ÷ 12 = 5 feet 6 inches. Step 4 – Add the two results together. 88 feet + 5 feet 6 inches = 93 feet 6 inches.

225) The correct answer is C. Since we are dealing with a square, all four sides of the floor are equal to each other. The tiles are also square, so they also have equal sides. Therefore, we can simply divide to get the answer: 64 ÷ 4 = 16

226) The correct answer is A. The volume of a cylinder is calculated as follows: volume ≈ 3.14 × (*radius*)^2 × *height* ≈ 3.14 × (5)^2 × 10 ≈ 785

227) The correct answer is A. First, we need to calculate the volume of cone A: (3.14 × 9^2 × 18) ÷ 3 = 1526.04. Then, we need to calculate the volume of Cone B: (3.14 × 3^2 × 6) ÷ 3 = 56.52. Then divide to get the ratio: 1526.04 ÷ 56.52 = 27. So, we can express the ratio as: $^{27}/_1$ = 27

228) The correct answer is C. Step 1 – Determine the cost from the first supplier: 500 × 0.72 = $360.00. The tax on this will be $360.00 × 5.5% = $19.80. Then add the tax to the cost to get the total: $360.00 + $19.80 = $379.80. Step 2 – Determine the total cost from the second supplier: $350 cost + ($350 × 0.055 tax) = $350 + 19.25 = $369.25. So, you will get the better deal from the second supplier at $369.25.

229) The correct answer is A. The range is the highest amount minus the lowest amount: 21 − 3 = 18

230) The correct answer is B. Two members have lost 12 kilograms, and all of the other amounts occur only one time each. So, 12 is the mode.

231) The correct answer is B. The line with the squares is the highest line for July. From the legend, we can see that this represents Company B.

232) The correct answer is C. The line with the diamonds represents Company A. The diamond symbol for April is nearly at the line for 8. The sales are represented in hundreds of thousands, so $790,000 is the best answer.

233) The correct answer is A. The line with the square for company B is at $1,400,000 for May. The line with the triangle for Company C is at $600,000 for May. So, Company B's sales were $800,000 more than Company C's for May.

234) The correct answer is A. We can see that December has the highest figure for all three of the lines. Accordingly, December will also have the greatest combined sales for all three companies.

235) The correct answer is D. We can see that SUV's account for the lowest number of accidents on each of the two dates. So, SUV's will also account for the lowest combined total for the two dates.

236) The correct answer is A. The chart shows that cars account for the largest number of accidents on each of the four dates represented. So, cars will also account for the largest combined total for all four dates.

237) The correct answer is C. Vans were involved in 12 accidents on March 1, and SUV's were involved in 8 accidents on the same date. So, vans and SUV's had 20 accidents in total on this date.

238) The correct answer is D. On May 1, pick-ups were involved in 7 accidents, and on June 1, they were involved in 10 accidents. So, for the two dates combined, pick-ups had 17 accidents.

239) The correct answer is C. Public safety and education were the highest, so add them together to solve: 21% + 27% = 48%

240) The correct answer is D. Take the total dollar amount and multiply by the 27% for education:
$5,275,300 × 0.27 = $1,424,331

241) The correct answer is C. Take the total dollar amount and multiply by the 21% for public safety:
$6,537,200 × 0.21 = $1,372,812

242) The correct answer is B. Substitute the values into the equation to solve. For $x = 2$ and $y = 3$:
$10x + 3y = (10 \times 2) + (3 \times 3) = 20 + 9 = 29$

243) The correct answer is B. Put the values provided for x into the second function. $f_2(9) = \sqrt{9} + 3 = 3 + 3 = 6$. Then put this result into the first function. $f_1(6) = 3 \times 6 + 1 = 19$

244) The correct answer is D. Multiply the radical in front of the parentheses by each radical inside the parentheses. Then simplify further if possible.
$\sqrt{6} \cdot (\sqrt{40} + \sqrt{6}) =$
$(\sqrt{6} \times \sqrt{40}) + (\sqrt{6} \times \sqrt{6}) =$
$\sqrt{240} + 6 = \sqrt{16 \times 15} + 6 = 4\sqrt{15} + 6$

245) The correct answer is C.
FIRST: **(x** – 9y)(**x** – 9y) = x × x = x^2
OUTSIDE: (**x** – 9y)(x – **9y**) = x × –9y = –9xy
INSIDE: (x – **9y**)(**x** – 9y) = –9y × x = –9xy
LAST: (x – **9y**)(x – **9y**) = –9y × –9y = $81y^2$
SOLUTION: $x^2 - 18xy + 81y^2$

246) The correct answer is B. Deal with the whole numbers first.
$6 + \frac{x}{4} \geq 22$
$6 - 6 + \frac{x}{4} \geq 22 - 6$
$\frac{x}{4} \geq 16$

Then eliminate the fraction.

$\frac{x}{4} \geq 16$

$4 \times \frac{x}{4} \geq 16 \times 4$

$x \geq 64$

247) The correct answer is A. Perform long division of the polynomial.

```
              x + 3
         _____
x – 4 ) x² – x – 12
        x² – 4x
        _____
             3x – 12
             3x – 12
             _____
                   0
```

248) The correct answer is A. Factor out xy: $18xy - 24x^2y - 48y^2x^2 = xy(18 - 24x - 48xy)$
Then, factor out the common factor of 6: $xy(18 - 24x - 48xy) = 6xy(3 - 4x - 8xy)$

249) The correct answer is C. Multiply the integers and add the exponents on the variables:

$\sqrt{15x^3} \times \sqrt{8x^2} =$

$\sqrt{15x^3 \times 8x^2} =$

$\sqrt{15 \times 8 \times x^3 \times x^2} =$

$\sqrt{120x^5} = \sqrt{2 \times 2 \times x^2 \times x^2 \times x \times 30} = 2x^2\sqrt{30x}$

250) The correct answer is A. Put in the values of 4 for x and –3 for y and simplify.

$2x^2 + 5xy - y^2 =$

$(2 \times 4^2) + (5 \times 4 \times -3) - (-3^2) =$

$(2 \times 4 \times 4) + (5 \times 4 \times -3) - (-3 \times -3) =$

$(2 \times 16) + (20 \times -3) - (9) =$

$32 + (-60) - 9 =$

$32 - 60 - 9 =$

$32 - 69 = -37$

TABE 9 & 10 Practice Test 3 – Solutions and Explanations

251) The correct answer is D. Convert the cups to quarter cups: 10 cups = 40 quarter cups. Then combine the whole number with the fraction and multiply to solve: 40¼ × 50 cents per quarter cup = 40.25 × 0.50 = $20.50

252) The correct answer is C. The problem is asking for the total for all five months, so we add the amounts together to solve: $723 + $618 + $576 + $812 + $984 = $3,713

253) The correct answer is C. Step 1 – Take the total number of employees and divide this by 5: 250 ÷ 5 = 50. Step 2 – The question asks how many questionnaires have not been completed and returned, so subtract to find the amount in the 'not returned' subset: 5 – 4 = 1. Step 3 – Multiply the result from step 2 by the result from step 1 to solve: 50 × 1 = 50

254) The correct answer is D. Step 1 – Determine the total for sales in December: $20 × 55 = $1,100. Step 2 – Determine the total sales for January: $12 × 20 = $240. Step 3 – Add these two amounts to solve: $1,100 + $240 = $1,340

255) The correct answer is A. The problem tells us that the morning flight had 52 passengers more than the evening flight, and there were 540 passengers in total on the two flights that day. Step 1 – First of all, we need to deduct the difference from the total: 540 – 52 = 488. In other words, there were 488 passengers on both flights combined, plus the 52 additional passengers on the morning flight.
Step 2 – Now divide this result by 2 to allocate an amount of passengers to each flight: 488 ÷ 2 = 244 passengers on the evening flight. (Had the question asked you for the amount of passengers on the morning flight, you would have had to add back the amount of additional passengers to find the total amount of passengers for the morning flight: 244 + 52 = 296 passengers on the morning flight)

256) The correct answer is C. Divide and then round up: 82 people in total ÷ 15 people served per container = 5.467 containers. We need to round up to 6 since we cannot purchase a fractional part of a container.

257) The correct answer is D. The question is asking us about a time duration of 6 minutes, so we need to calculate the amount of seconds in 6 minutes: 6 minutes × 60 seconds per minute = 360 seconds in total. Then divide the total time by the amount of time needed to make one journey: 360 seconds ÷ 45 seconds per journey = 8 journeys. Finally, multiply the number of journeys by the amount of inches per journey in order to get the total inches: 10.5 inches for 1 journey × 8 journeys = 84 inches in total

258) The correct answer is B. First of all, add up to find the total number of customers: 40 + 30 + 20 + 30 = 120 customers in total for all four regions. The salespeople received $540 in total, so we need to divide this by the amount of customers: $540 ÷ 120 customers = $4.50 per customer

259) The correct answer is B. The mean is the arithmetic average. First, find the total for all seven companies: –2% + 5% + 7.5% + 14% + 17% + 1.3% + –3% = 39.8%. Then divide by 7 since there are 7 companies in the set: 39.8% ÷ 7 = 5.68% ≈ 5.7%

260) The correct answer is D. The plumber is going to earn $4,000 for the month. He charges a set fee of $100 per job, and he will do 5 jobs, so we can calculate the total set fees first: $100 set fee per job × 5 jobs = $500 total set fees. Then deduct the set fees from the total for the month in order to determine the total for the hourly pay: $4,000 – $500 = $3,500. He earns $25 per hour, so divide the hourly rate into the total hourly pay in order to determine the number of hours he will work: $3,500 total hourly pay ÷ $25 per hour = 140 hours to work

261) The correct answer is A. Set up each part of the problem as an equation. The museum had twice as many visitors on Tuesday (T) as on Monday (M), so T = 2M. The number of visitors on Wednesday exceeded that of Tuesday by 20%, so W = 1.20 × T. Then express T in terms of M for Wednesday's

visitors: W = 1.20 × T = 1.20 × 2M = 2.40M. Finally, add the amounts together for all three days: M + 2M + 2.40M = 5.4M

262) The correct answer is B. 45% of the freshman, 30% of the sophomores, 38% of the juniors, and 30% of the seniors will attend. Since each of the four grade levels has roughly the same number of students, we can simply divide by 4 to get the average. Calculating the average, we get the overall percentage for all four grades: (45 + 30 + 38 + 30) ÷ 4 = 35.75%. 35% is the closest answer to 35.75%, so it best approximates our result.

263) The correct answer is C. Step 1 – Determine the commission earned per hour: $15 charged – $12 paid to employee = $3 per hour commission. Step 2 – Calculate the total hours that the 10 employees worked: 10 × 40 = 400 hours in total. Step 3 – Multiply the total number of hours by the commission per hour to solve: 400 hours × $3 commission per hour = $1,200 total commission

264) The correct answer is D. Divide to solve: 49 ÷ 50 = 0.98 = 98%

265) The correct answer is D. Calculate the total, and divide by the number of days. Step 1 – Find the total: $90 + $85 + $85 + $105 + $110 = $475. Step 2 – Divide the result from Step 1 by the number of days: $475 ÷ 5 = $95

266) The correct answer is D. Step 1 – Add the whole numbers: 8 + 7 = 15. Step 2 – Add the fractions: 3/4 + 1/2 = 3/4 + 2/4 = 5/4. Step 3 – Simplify the fraction from Step 2: 5/4 = 4/4 + 1/4 = $1^{1}/_{4}$ = 1 foot and 3 inches. Step 4 – Combine the results from Step 1 and Step 3 to solve the problem: 15 feet + 1 foot and 3 inches = 16 feet and 3 inches

267) The correct answer is C. In this problem, the fraction on the second number is larger than the fraction on the first number, so we need to convert the first fraction before we start our calculation. Step 1 – Convert $28^{3}/_{10}$ for subtraction: $28^{3}/_{10}$ = $27^{3}/_{10}$ + 1 = $27^{3}/_{10}$ + $^{10}/_{10}$ = $27^{13}/_{10}$. Step 2 – Subtract the whole numbers. $7^{9}/_{10}$ hours have been spent on the job so far, so subtract the 7 hours: 27 – 7 = 20. Step 3 – Subtract the fractions: 13/10 – 9/10 = 4/10. Step 4 – Simplify the fraction from Step 3: 4/10 = (4 ÷ 2)/(10 ÷ 2) = 2/5. Step 4 – Combine the results from Step 2 and Step 4 to get your new mixed number to solve the problem: 20 + 2/5 = $20^{2}/_{5}$

268) The correct answer is C. Step 1 – Take the 147 parts of blue slate chippings for this order and divide by the 3 parts stated in the original ratio: 147 ÷ 3 = 49. Step 2 – Multiply the result from Step 1 by the 2 parts of white gravel stated in the original ratio to get your answer: 49 × 2 = 98

269) The correct answer is C. Step 1 – Determine the total amount of inches of material needed for one unit. Don't forget that the second material needs to be doubled because there is a double layer of this material: 18 + 19 + 19 = 56 inches. Step 2 – Calculate how many inches are needed in total: 56 inches per unit × 18 units = 1008 inches in total. Step 3 – Convert the inches to feet: 1008 inches ÷ 12 = 84 feet

270) The correct answer is D. Step 1 – Determine the excess amount over the amount for the deal: 100 bottles needed – (4 cases × 24 bottles each) = 100 – 96 = 4 individual bottles left. Step 2 – Take the result from the previous step and multiply by the individual price: 4 × $2.50 = $10. Step 3 – Determine the cost of the 4 cases: 4 × $50 = $200. Step 4 – Add the results from the previous two steps to get the total wholesale price for the deal: $200 + $10 = $210

271) The correct answer is A. Step 1 – Convert the grams to ounces: 1190.7 ÷ 28.35 = 42. Step 2 – Add the result from step 1 to the amount of ounces for the US order to solve: 39 + 42 = 81 ounces

272) The correct answer is B. Step 1 – Find the area of the ceiling. The formula for the area of a rectangle is (length × width). So, substitute the values to find the area: (35 × 25) = 875 square feet. Step 2 – Find the area of each ceiling tile. The measurements for our tiles are given in inches: 6 inches by 6 inches = 36 square inches. Step 3 – Calculate how many square inches there are in a square foot: 12

inches by 12 inches = 144 square inches. Step 4 – Determine how many tiles you need per square foot: 144 square inches ÷ 36 square inches per tile = 4 tiles per square foot. Step 5 – Multiply to solve: 875 square feet in total × 4 tiles per square foot = 3,500 tiles needed

273) The correct answer is B. From the formula sheet, we can see that 1 milligram = 0.001 gram. We are converting milligrams to grams, so we are doing the formula in the correct order, rather than in reverse. Therefore, multiply by 0.001 to solve: 1,275,000 milligrams × 0.001 = 1,275 grams

274) The correct answer is D. Step 1 – Find the radius in centimeters. The diameter is 10 inches, so the radius is 5 inches. 1 inch = 2.54 centimeters, so multiply to determine the length of the radius in centimeters: 5 × 2.54 = 12.7 centimeters. Step 2 – Cube the radius for the formula: 12.7 × 12.7 × 12.7 = 2048.38. Then multiply by 3.14 and 4/3 to find the volume of the sphere: 2048.38 × 3.14 × 4/3 = 8575.8968, which we round up to 8,576.

275) The correct answer is B. To calculate a reverse percentage you need to divide, rather than multiply. So, take the $12 retail price and divide by 625%, which is 100% for the cost plus 525% for the markup: $12 ÷ 625% = $12 ÷ 6.25 = $1.92

276) The correct answer is D. The perimeter of rectangle is 2(*length* + *width*). So, determine the total width for both sides: 2 × 75 = 150. Now deduct this amount from the perimeter: 350 – 150 = 200. Finally, divide this result by 2 to get the length: 200 ÷ 2 = 100

277) The correct answer is D. Step 1 – Calculate the cubic inches for each box: length × width × height = 3 × 3 × 2 = 18 cubic feet per box × 1,728 cubic inches per cubic foot = 31,104 cubic inches per box. Step 2 – Determine how much of the product is on hand. The first box is 1/6 full, the second box is 1/2 full, and the third box is 2/3 full: 1/6 + 1/2 + 2/3 = 1/6 + 3/6 + 4/6 = 8/6 .= 12/6 = 1 1/3 boxes left. Step 3 – Determine how much is required to replenish the stock: 3 boxes needed – 1 1/3 boxes on hand = 1 2/3 boxes needed. Step 4 – Determine how many cubic inches are needed: 1 2/3 boxes needed × 31,104 cubic inches per box = 51,840 cubic inches needed. Step 5 – Calculate the cost of the cubic inches: 51,840 cubic inches needed × 0.09 per cubic inch = $4,665.60, which we round to $4,666.

278) The correct answer is B. This question is asking you to determine the value missing from a sample space when calculating basic probability. This is like other problems on basic probability, but we need to work backwards to find the missing value. First, set up an equation to find the total items in the sample space. Then subtract the quantities of the known subsets from the total in order to determine the missing value. We will use variable T as the total number of items in the set. The probability of getting a red ribbon is 1/3.

So, set up an equation to find the total items in the data set:

$$\frac{5}{T} = \frac{1}{3}$$

$$\frac{5}{T} \times 3 = \frac{1}{3} \times 3$$

$$\frac{5}{T} \times 3 = 1$$

$$\frac{15}{T} = 1$$

$$\frac{15}{T} \times T = 1 \times T$$

$15 = T$

We have 5 red ribbons, 6 blue ribbons, and x green ribbons in the data set that make up the total sample space, so now subtract the amount of red and blue ribbons from the total in order to determine the number of green ribbons.
$5 + 6 + x = 15$
$11 + x = 15$
$11 - 11 + x = 15 - 11$
$x = 4$

279) The correct answer is B. Our data set is: 2.5, 9.4, 3.1, 1.7, 3.2, 8.2, 4.5, 6.4, 7.8. First, put the numbers in ascending order: 1.7, 2.5, 3.1, 3.2, 4.5, 6.4, 7.8, 8.2, 9.4. The median is the number in the middle of the set: 1.7, 2.5, 3.1, 3.2, **4.5**, 6.4, 7.8, 8.2, 9.4

280) The correct answer is A. Count the sides of the squares on the gray part of the diagram: Left = 5; Bottom = 3 + 1 = 4, Right = 2 + 3 = 5; Top = 4. Then add up: 5 + 4 + 5 + 4 = 18. Alternatively, visually go around the gray figure and count up the outside edges of the gray squares.

281) The correct answer is C. First, calculate the total area represented on the diagram: 9 × 7 = 63 square yards in total. Then count the gray squares for the reservoir. We can see that there are 18 gray squares. Then subtract to solve: 63 – 18 = 45 square yards

282) The correct answer is A. We know from the calculations in the answer to the previous question that the gray area is 18 square yards and the white area is 45 square yards. So, the ratio is 18:45. Both of these numbers are divisible by 9, so we can simplify the ratio to 2:5 (18 ÷ 9 = 2 and 45 ÷ 9 = 5)

283) The correct answer is D. Calculate the length of strapping for the piece that goes over the front of the package: 22 + 42 + 22 + 42 = 128. Then calculate the length of strapping for the piece that goes over the top of the package: 20 + 42 + 20 + 42 = 124. Then add the 15 inches for the handle: 128 + 124 + 15 = 267 total inches

284) The correct answer is C. We know from the calculations in the answer to the previous question that without the handle, we need 128 + 124 = 252 inches per package. 252 inches per package × 25 packages = 6,300 total inches

285) The correct answer is C. To calculate cubic inches, we take the height times the depth times the length: 20 × 22 × 42 = 18,480 cubic inches

286) The correct answer is D. Part 3 had 35 total questions and part 4 had 45 total questions, so add to solve: 35 + 45 = 80

287) The correct answer is A. Chantelle correctly answered 12 out of 15 questions, so she incorrectly answered 3 questions (15 – 12 = 3). This can be expressed as the fraction 3/15, which can be simplified to 1/5.

288) The correct answer is B. First calculate how many correct answers there were: 12 + 20 + 32 + 32 = 96. Then calculate how many questions were on the test in total: 15 + 25 + 35 + 45 = 120. Finally, divide to solve 96 ÷ 120 = 0.80 = 80%

289) The correct answer is D. Try to find the pattern of relationship between the numbers. Here, we can see that: 2 × 2 = 4; 4 × 2 = 8; 8 × 2 = 16. In other words, the next number in the sequence is always double the previous number. Therefore the answer is: 16 × 2 = 32

290) The correct answer is C.
Here is the solution for y intercept:
$5x^2 + 4y^2 = 120$
$5(0)^2 + 4y^2 = 120$
$0 + 4y^2 = 120$
$4y^2 = 120$
$4y^2 \div 4 = 120 \div 4$
$y^2 = 30$
$y = \sqrt{30}$
So, the y intercept is $(0, \sqrt{30})$

Here is the solution for x intercept:
$5x^2 + 4y^2 = 120$
$5x^2 + 4(0)^2 = 120$
$5x^2 + 0 = 120$
$5x^2 = 120$
$5x^2 \div 5 = 120 \div 5$
$x^2 = \sqrt{24}$
So the x intercept is $(\sqrt{24}, 0)$

291) The correct answer is B. Use the slope-intercept formula to calculate the slope: $y = mx + b$, where m is the slope and b is the y intercept. In our question, $x = 4$ and $y = 15$. The line crosses the y axis at 3, so put the values into the formula.
$y = mx + b$
$15 = m4 + 3$
$15 - 3 = m4 + 3 - 3$
$12 = m4$
$12 \div 4 = m$
$3 = m$

292) The correct answer is B. Substitute 8 for x to solve.
$x^2 - 5x - 9 =$
$8^2 - (5 \times 8) - 9 =$
$64 - 40 - 9 =$
15

293) The correct answer is A. Get rid of the integer on the left by adding 9 to each side of the equation.
$5x - 9 = 6$
$5x - 9 + 9 = 6 + 9$
$5x = 15$
Then divide each side by 5 to isolate x and solve.
$5x \div 5 = 15 \div 5$
$x = 3$

294) The correct answer is D. Divide each side of the equation by 3. Then subtract 5 from both sides of the equation as shown below.
$18 = 3(x + 5)$
$18 \div 3 = [3(x + 5)] \div 3$
$6 = x + 5$
$6 - 5 = x + 5 - 5$
$1 = x$

295) The correct answer is B. $y^x = Z$ is the same as $x = \log_y Z$, so $9^2 = 81$ is the same as $2 = \log_9 81$.

296) The correct answer is C. In order to multiply two square roots, multiply the numbers inside the radical signs: $\sqrt{5} \times \sqrt{3} = \sqrt{5 \times 3} = \sqrt{15}$

297) The correct answer is B. Find the lowest common denominator. Then add the numerators together as shown: $\frac{x}{5} + \frac{y}{2} = \left(\frac{x}{5} \times \frac{2}{2}\right) + \left(\frac{y}{2} \times \frac{5}{5}\right) = \frac{2x}{10} + \frac{5y}{10} = \frac{2x + 5y}{10}$

298) The correct answer is D. Place the integers on one side of the inequality.
$-3x + 14 < 5$
$-3x + 14 - 14 < 5 - 14$
$-3x < -9$
Then get rid of the negative number. We need to reverse the way that the inequality sign points because we are dividing by a negative.
$-3x < -9$
$-3x \div -3 > -9 \div -3$ ("Less than" becomes "greater than" because we divide by a negative number.)
$x > 3$
3.15 is greater than 3, so it is the correct answer.

299) The correct answer is A.
FIRST: $(x - 2y)(2x^2 - y) = x \times 2x^2 = 2x^3$
OUTSIDE: $(x - 2y)(2x^2 - y) = x \times -y = -xy$
INSIDE: $(x - 2y)(2x^2 - y) = -2y \times 2x^2 = -4x^2y$
LAST: $(x - 2y)(2x^2 - y) = -2y \times -y = 2y^2$
SOLUTION: $2x^3 + - xy + - 4x^2y + 2y^2 = 2x^3 - 4x^2y + 2y^2 - xy$

300) The correct answer is D. Isolate the whole numbers to one side of the equation first.
$20 - \frac{3x}{4} \geq 17$
$(20 - 20) - \frac{3x}{4} \geq 17 - 20$
$-\frac{3x}{4} \geq -3$
Then get rid of the fraction.
$-\frac{3x}{4} \geq -3$
$\left(4 \times -\frac{3x}{4}\right) \geq -3 \times 4$
$-3x \geq -12$

Then deal with the remaining whole numbers.
$-3x \geq -12$
$-3x \div -3 \geq -12 \div -3$
$x \leq 4$
Remember to reverse the way the sign points when you divide by a negative number.

TABE 9 & 10 Practice Test 4 – Solutions and Explanations

301) The correct answer is C. The question is asking for the change from week 3 to week 4, so subtract week 3 from week 4 as shown: −5 − (−12) = −5 + 12 = 7

302) The correct answer is C. The problem states that the salesperson gets a $12 commission for every order greater than $100, so we need to multiply the amount of the commission by the number of orders over $100 first of all: $12 × 32 = $384. Then add this to the basic pay to get the total for the month: $1250 + $384 = $1634

303) The correct answer is B. Divide the total amount of sales by the price per unit to solve: $310 ÷ $12.40 = 25 units sold

304) The correct answer is D. The ratio of bags of apples to bags of oranges is 2 to 3, so for every two bags of apples, there are three bags of oranges. First, take the total amount of bags of apples and divide by the 2 from the original ratio: 44 ÷ 2 = 22. Then multiply this by 3 to determine how many bags of oranges are in the store: 22 × 3 = 66

305) The correct answer is B. At the beginning of January, there are 300 students, but 5% of the students leave during the month, so we have 95% left at the end of the month: 300 × 95% = 285. Then 15 students join on the last day of the month, so we add that back in to get the total at the end of January: 285 + 15 = 300. If this pattern continues, there will always be 300 students in the academy at the end of any month.

306) The correct answer is D. Calculate the discount: $120 × 12.5% = $15 discount. Then subtract the discount from the original price to determine the sales price: $120 − $15 = $105

307) The correct answer is A. The ratio of defective chips to functioning chips is 1 to 20. So, the defective chips form one group and the functioning chips form another group. Therefore, the total data set can be divided into groups of 21. Accordingly, $1/21$ of the chips will be defective. The factory produced 11,235 chips last week, so we calculate as follows: 11,235 × $1/21$ = 535

308) The correct answer is B. The total amount available is $55,000, so we can substitute this for C in the equation provided in order to calculate R number of residents:
C = $750R + $2,550
$55,000 = $750R + $2,550
$55,000 − $2,550 = $750R + $2,550 − $2,550
$55,000 − $2,550 = $750R
$52,450 = $750R
$52,450 ÷ $750 = $750R ÷ $750
$52,450 ÷ $750 = R
69.9 = R
It is not possible to accommodate a fractional part of one person, so we need to round down to 69 residents.

309) The correct answer is B. Our data set is: 2.5, 9.4, 3.1, 1.7, 3.2, 8.2, 4.5, 6.4, 7.8. First, put the numbers in ascending order: 1.7, 2.5, 3.1, 3.2, 4.5, 6.4, 7.8, 8.2, 9.4. The median is the number in the middle of the set: 1.7, 2.5, 3.1, 3.2, **4.5**, 6.4, 7.8, 8.2, 9.4

310) The correct answer is D. To find the mean, add up all of the items in the set and then divide by the number of items in the set. Here we have 7 numbers in the set, so we get our answer as follows:
(89 + 65 + 75 + 68 + 82 + 74 + 86) ÷ 7 = 539 ÷ 7 = 77

311) The correct answer is A. We don't know the age of the 8th car, so put this in as x to solve:
$(2 + 3 + 4 + 5 + 9 + 10 + 12 + x) \div 8 = 6$
$[(2 + 3 + 4 + 5 + 9 + 10 + 12 + x) \div 8] \times 8 = 6 \times 8$
$2 + 3 + 4 + 5 + 9 + 10 + 12 + x = 48$
$45 + x = 48$
$x = 3$

312) The correct answer is C. The fine for speeding is $50 per violation, so the total amount collected for speeding violations was: 60 speeding violations × $50 per violation = $3000. There 90 other violations, and the fine for other violations is $20, so the total for other violations is: 90 × $20 = $1800. Next, we need to deduct these two amounts from the total collections of $6,000 in order to find out how much was collected for parking violations: $6000 − $3000 − $1800 = $1200 in total for parking violations. There were 30 parking violations. We divide to get the answer: $1200 income for parking violations ÷ 30 parking violations = $40 each

313) The correct answer is B. The original price of the sofa on Wednesday was x. On Thursday, the sofa was reduced by 10%, so the price on Thursday was 90% of x or $0.90x$. On Friday, the sofa was reduced by a further 15%, so the price on Friday was 85% of the price on Thursday, so we can multiply Thursday's price by 0.85 to get our answer: $(0.90)(0.85)x$

314) The correct answer is C. If the amount earned from selling jackets was one-third that of selling jeans, the ratio of jacket to jean sales was 1 to 3. So, we need to divide the total sales of $4,000 into $1,000 for jackets and $3,000 for jeans. We can then solve the problem as follows: $3,000 in jeans sales ÷ $20 per pair = 150 pairs sold

315) The correct answer is D. Move the decimal point two places to the left and remove the percent sign: 81% = 81 ÷ 100 = 0.81

316) The correct answer is A. Step 1 – Add the whole numbers: 37 + 25 = 62. Step 2 – Add the fractions: 2/5 + 4/5 = 6/5 = 1 1/5. Step 3 – Combine the results from Step 1 and Step 2 to get your new mixed number to solve the problem: 62 + 1 1/5 = 63 1/5

317) The correct answer is C. Step 1 – Take the total amount of customers expected and divide by the 3 stated in the original ratio: 15 ÷ 3 = 5. Step 2 – Take the amount from Step 1 and multiply by 1 from the original ratio to solve the problem: 5 × 1 = 5

318) The correct answer is D. Step 1 – Calculate the amount of time spent on the initial job: 9:15 AM to 10:25 AM = 1 hour and 10 minutes = 70 minutes. Step 2 – Calculate the rate per square yard: 70 minutes ÷ 7 square yards = 10 minutes per square yard. Step 3 – Multiply the figure from Step 2 by the total amount of square yards to paint: 17.5 square yards × 10 minutes per square yard = 175 minutes = 2 hours and 55 minutes. Step 4 – Determine the time of completion: 9:15 AM + 2 hours and 55 minutes = 11:15 AM + 55 minutes = 12:10 PM

319) The correct answer is A. Add the three figures together to solve: 1235.35 + 567.55 + 347.25 = 2150.15 units

320) The correct answer is D. Step 1 – Add the whole numbers: 19 + 14 = 33. Step 2 – Add the fractions: 3/4 + 3/4 = 6/4. Step 3 – Simplify the fraction from Step 2: 6/4 = 1 2/4 = 1 1/2. Step 4 – Combine the results from Step 1 and Step 3 to solve the problem: 33 + 1 1/2 = 34 1/2

321) The correct answer is A. In this problem, the fraction on the second number is larger than the fraction on the first number, so we need to convert the first fraction before we start our calculation. Step 1 – Convert the first mixed number for subtraction: $102 \, 7/18 = 101 \, 7/18 + 1 = 101 \, 7/18 + 18/18 = 101 \, 25/18$. Step 2 – Subtract the whole numbers: 101 − 24 = 77. Step 3 – Subtract the fractions: 25/18 − 11/18 =

14/18. Step 4 – Simplify the fraction from Step 3: 14/18 = (14 ÷ 2)/(18 ÷ 2) = 7/9. Step 5 – Combine the results from Step 2 and Step 4 to get your new mixed number to solve the problem: 77 + 7/9 = 77⁷/₉.

322) The correct answer is C. Step 1 – Convert the mixed number to minutes: $1^3/_4$ = 1 hour and 45 minutes = 105 minutes. Step 2 – Multiply the 15 minutes by the 14 patients: 15 × 14 = 210 minutes. Step 3 – Add the results from steps 1 and 2: 105 + 210 = 315 minutes. Step 4 – Calculate how many minutes there are in 8 hours × 60 = 480 minutes. Step 5 – Determine how much time is left: 480 minutes available – 315 minutes on tasks = 165 minutes left. Step 6 – Convert this to hours an minutes: hours: 165 minutes = 2 hours and 45 minutes

323) The correct answer is D. Calculate the total, and divide by the number of employees. Step 1 – Find the total: 96 + 89 + 63 + 98 + 81 + 77 = 504. Step 2 – Divide the result from Step 1 by the number of employees: 504 ÷ 6 = 84

324) The correct answer is D. Circumference ≈ diameter × 3.14. The circumference of the first circle is calculated as follows: diameter × 3.14 = 10 × 3.14 = 31.4. The circumference of the second circle is as follows: diameter × 3.14 = 6 × 3.14 = 18.84. The difference in the circumferences is: 31.4 – 18.84 = 12.56

325) The correct answer is B. The circumference of the large tire is 20 × 3.14 = 62.80, and the circumference of the smaller tire is 12 × 3.14 = 37.68. If the large tire travels 360 revolutions, it travels a distance of approximately 22,608, since 62.80 × 360 = 22,608. To determine the number of revolutions the small tire needs to make to go the same distance, we divide the distance by the circumference of the smaller tire: 22,608 ÷ 37.68 = 600. Finally, calculate the difference in the number of revolutions: 600 – 360 = 240

326) The correct answer is C. Perimeter = 2L + 2W = (2 × 18) + (2 × 10) = 36 + 20 = 56

327) The correct answer is C. The circumference of a circle is approximately 3.14 times the diameter. The partition is going to divide the circular arena in half, so the partition will be placed on the diameter of the circle. So divide to calculate the diameter in feet: 1,017.36 ÷ 3.14 = 324 feet. We need to express the result in yards, so divide by 3 to solve: 324 ÷ 3 = 108 yards

328) The correct answer is D. Step 1 – Determine the percentage of the discount on Product A: $4 discount ÷ $20 original price = 20% discount. Step 2 – Calculate the dollar value of the discount on Product B: $16 × 20% = $3.20. Step 3 – Subtract the dollar value of the discount on Product B from the normal price to get the discounted price of Product B: $16 - $3.20 = $12.80

329) The correct answer is A. Step 1 – First we need to calculate the volume in terms of cubic inches. 10 inches × 7 inches × 5 inches = 350 cubic inches. Step 2 – Convert the cubic inches to gallons. 1 gallon = 231 cubic inches, so divide by 231 to get the gallons: 350 ÷ 231 = 1.5151 gallons, which we round to 1.52 gallons.

330) The correct answer is D. Step 1 – Take the 14 cups for this batch and divide by the 2 cups stated in the original ratio: 14 ÷ 2 = 7. Step 2 – Multiply the result from Step 1 by the 3 ounces of herbal therapy product stated in the original ratio to get your answer: 3 × 7 = 21

331) The correct answer is C. Step 1 – Convert the mixed number to a decimal: $1^1/_4$ = 1.25 hours. Step 2 – Multiply the result from the previous step by the number of intervals: 1.25 × 7 = 8.75 hours. Step 3 – Convert the decimal to minutes: 0.75 hour = 45 minutes. Step 4 – Express your answer in hours and minutes: 8 hours and 45 minutes

332) The correct answer is A. Find the amount of items in the sample set before anything is removed from the set: 4 + 2 + 1 + 4 + 5 = 16. One rope has been removed, so deduct that from the sample space for the second draw: 16 – 1 = 15. The box original had 4 pieces of blue rope, and one piece of blue rope has

been removed, so there are 3 pieces of blue rope available for the second draw. So, the probability is $3/15 = 1/5$

333) The correct answer is C. Three out of ten students are taking the class. So, here we have the proportion 3 to 10. Step 1 – Divide the total number of students by the second number in the proportion to get the number of groups: 650 ÷ 10 = 65 groups. Step 2 – Multiply the number of groups by the first number in the proportion in order to get the result: 3 × 65 = 195 art students.

334) The correct answer is D. Each journey lasts 46 minutes, so if the train arrives at 5:51 pm, it departs at 5:05 pm. (5:51 – 46 minutes = 5:05)

335) The correct answer is A. Each journey lasts 46 minutes, so if the train departs at 12:30 pm, it will arrive at 1:16 pm. (12:30 + 46 minutes = 1:16)

336) The correct answer is C. It is 46 minutes there and 46 minutes back, so the travel time for a round trip is 46 + 46 = 92 minutes, which is 1 hour and 32 minutes.

337) The correct answer is A. The temperature on Sunday was –10 and on Saturday it was 12, so we calculate the difference by subtracting Sunday from Saturday: 12 – (–10) = 12 + 10 = 22 degrees

338) The correct answer is C. Place the values for the temperatures in ascending order: –10, –9, 1, 6, 8 12, 13. The median is the one in the middle: –10, –9, 1, **6**, 8, 12, 13

339) The correct answer is B. Add up all of the values: –10 + –9 + 1 + 6 + 8 + 12 + 13 = 21. Then divide by 7 for the seven days represented: 21 ÷ 7 = 3

340) The correct answer is D. None of the values occurs more than once, so there is no mode.

341) The correct answer is D. The range is the high minus the low: 13 – (–10) = 23

342) The correct answer is C. The y intercept is where $x = 0$. So, we can substitute 0 in our equation to solve: ($12 + 2x$) ÷ (4 + x) = ($12 + 0) ÷ (4 + 0) = $12 ÷ 4 = 3.

343) The correct answer is B. If you try to find the difference between numbers by performing addition, you will quickly realize that you cannot solve the problem by addition. In this practice problem, each subsequent number in the sequence is found by dividing the previous number by 5 and then multiplying by –1. Alternatively, you can think of it as multiplying by $-1/5$ each time: $-1/5 \times -1/5 = 1/25$. So, the next term in the sequence is $1/25$.

344) The correct answer is D. Be careful with your zeroes. We are taking 340,000 (4 zeroes) times 1,000 (three zeroes). The result is: 340,000 × 1,000 = 340,000,000 = 34 × 10,000,000 (seven zeroes). However, our answer choices are expressed with 3.4, not 34. So, we will need to multiply by a figure with 8 zeroes to account for the change in the position of the decimal.
3.4×10^8 millimeters = 3.4 × 100,000,000 millimeters = 340,000,000

345) The correct answer is A. The problem tells us that A is 3 times B, and B is 3 more than 6 times C. So, we need to create equations based on this information.
B is 3 more than 6 times C: B = 6C + 3
A is 3 times B: A = 3B

Since B = 6C + 3, we can substitute 6C + 3 for B in the second equation as follows:
A = 3B
A = 3(6C + 3)
A = 18C + 9
So, A is 9 more than 18 times C.

346) The correct answer is D. Any negative exponent is equal to 1 divided by the variable. So, $x^{-4} = 1 \div x^4$

347) The correct answer is C. Deal with the integers that are outside the parentheses first. Then remove the radical to solve.
$5(4\sqrt{x} - 8) = 40$
$20\sqrt{x} - 40 = 40$
$20\sqrt{x} - 40 + 40 = 40 + 40$
$20\sqrt{x} = 80$
$20\sqrt{x} \div 20 = 80 \div 20$
$\sqrt{x} = 4$
$\sqrt{x}^2 = 4^2$
$x = 16$

348) The correct answer is A. Find the cube roots of the integers and factor them. Express the result as a rational number.

$$\sqrt[3]{\frac{8}{27}} = \sqrt[3]{\frac{2 \times 2 \times 2}{3 \times 3 \times 3}} = \frac{2}{3}$$

349) The correct answer is C. When you see numbers inside two lines like this, you are being asked for the absolute value. Absolute value is always a positive number. For example, | –7| = 7. So, first of all we need to perform the operation inside the absolute value signs. |5 – 8| = | –3| = 3. However, here we have a negative sign in front of the absolute value. Therefore, we need to make the result negative since there is a negative sign in front of the absolute value: – | 5 – 8| = – | –3| = – |3| = –3

350) The correct answer is D. $\sqrt{18} \times \sqrt{8} = \sqrt{18 \times 8} = \sqrt{144} = \sqrt{12 \times 12} = 12$

TABE 9 & 10 Practice Test 5 – Solutions and Explanations

351) The correct answer is D. Add the gains and subtract the setbacks as shown:
−14 + 52 − 36 − 7 = −5

352) The correct answer is C. Divide and then express the result as a percentage. Step 1 – Treat the line in the fraction as the division symbol: 9/16 = 9 ÷ 16 = 0.5625. Step 2 – To express the result from Step 1 as a percentage, move the decimal point two places to the right and add the percent sign: 0.5625 = 56.25%

353) The correct answer is C. Move the decimal point two places to the right and add the percent sign: 0.95 = 95.0%

354) The correct answer is B. Subtract the decimal from 1 to find the decimal amount left: 1 − 0.05 = 0.95. Then multiply the total number of employees at the start of the year by this decimal number: 120 × 0.95 = 114 employees left

355) The correct answer is D. 20 percent is equal to 0.20. We are doing a reverse percentage, so we need to divide to solve: $60 ÷ 0.20 = $300. We can check this result as follows: 300 × 0.20 = 60

356) The correct answer is A. First, subtract whole numbers: 6 − 2 = 4. Then subtract fractions: $3/4 - 1/2 = 3/4 - 2/4 = 1/4$. Put them together for the result: $4 1/4$

357) The correct answer is B. Set up the proportion as a fraction: 9 ounces of liquid for every 6 of ounces active chemical = $9/6$. Then simplify the fraction: $9/6 ÷ 3/3 = 3/2$. Now, multiply the fraction by the amount for the current job to solve: $3/2 × 10 = 30/2 = 30 ÷ 2 = 15$

358) The correct answer is B. First you need to find the total points. You do this by taking the erroneous average times 5: 5 × 96 = 480. Then you need to divide the total points earned by the correct number of surveys to get the correct average: 480 ÷ 6 = 80

359) The correct answer is C. You have 3 partial trays of unsold brownies at the end of the day, and each tray has $1/8$ of the brownies left in it, so in total you have $3/8$ of a tray left. You need to divide this by 4 employees. When you are asked to divide fractions, remember that you need to invert the second fraction. Here we have the whole number 4. 4 inverted is $1/4$. So, multiply the fractions to solve: $3/8 × 1/4 = (3 × 1)/(8 × 4) = 3/32$

360) The correct answer is A. Represent the mixed numbers as decimal numbers: Person 1: $14 3/4$ = 14.75; Person 2: $20 1/5$ = 20.20; Person 3: 36.35. Then add all three amounts together to find the total: 14.75 + 20.20 + 36.35 = 71.30

361) The correct answer is C. The office purchased 50 reams of paper this month and has used 5 of them, so you need to divide to solve 5 ÷ 50 = 0.10

362) The correct answer is D. First of all, you have to calculate the total amount of points earned by the entire group. Multiply the female average by the amount of female candidates. Total points for females: 87 × 55 = 4785. Then multiply the male average by the amount of males. Total points for male candidates: 80 × 45 = 3600. Then add these two amounts together to find out the total points scored by the entire group. Total points for entire group: 4785 + 3600 = 8385. When you have calculated the total amount of points for the entire group, you divide this by the total number of candidates to get the average: 8385 ÷ 100 = 83.35

363) The correct answer is A. We know that Mary has already gotten 80% of the money. However, the question is asking how much money she still needs: 100% − 80% = 20% = 0.20. Now do the multiplication: 650 × 0.20 = 130

364) The correct answer is B. They buy 4 of product A at $5 each, so they buy $20 worth of product A. They paid $60 in total, so subtract the total cost of product A from the overall total to calculate the total spent on Product B: $60 − $20 = $40. Product B costs $8 each, so divide to solve: $40 spent on Product B ÷ $8 each = 5 units

365) The correct answer is C. She bought 3 pairs of shoes, so determine the amount spent on shoes: 3 pairs of shoes × $25 each= $75. Then deduct this from the total amount of the purchase to calculate how much she spent on socks: $85 − $75 = $10. The socks cost $2 a pair, so divide to solve: $10 ÷ $2 each = 5 pairs

366) The correct answer is C. Step 1 – Determine the price per yard: $10.50 per 1/2 yard × 2 = $21.00 per yard. Step 2 – Calculate the price for 20 yards: 20 × $21.00 = $420.00. Step 3 – The customer purchased 20 and a half yards, so the price of the remaining half yard is $10.50. Add this to the result from Step 2 to get your answer: $420.00 + $10.50 = $430.50

367) The correct answer is D. Step 1 – Add the whole numbers: 49 + 18 = 67. Step 2 – Add the fractions: 3/16 + 1/16 = 4/16 = 1/4. Step 3 – Combine the results from Step 1 and Step 2 to get your new mixed number to solve the problem: 67 + 1/4 = 67 1/4

368) The correct answer is B. Take the amount of defective SIM cards and divide by the total amount of SIM cards: 11 ÷ 132 = 0.083 = 8.3%, which we round to 8%.

369) The correct answer is A. Step 1 – Take the total amount of flour required for this batch and divide by the 9 stated in the original ratio: 126 ÷ 9 = 14. Step 2 – Take the amount from Step 1 and multiply by 2 from the original ratio to solve the problem: 14 × 2 = 28

370) The correct answer is B. Step 1 – Calculate the amount of time spent on the initial job: 12:10 to 2:25 = 2 hours and 15 minutes = 135 minutes. Step 2 – Calculate the rate per cap: 135 minutes ÷ 3 caps = 45 minutes per cap. Step 3 – Calculate how many minutes there are in 9 hours: 9 hours × 60 minutes = 540 minutes. Step 4 – Divide to solve: 540 minutes available ÷ 45 minutes per cap = 12 caps

371) The correct answer is D. Add the percentages together to solve: 58% + 27% = 85%

372) The correct answer is C. The circumference of a circle is calculated by using this formula: Circumference ≈ 3.14 × diameter. The diameter of a circle is always equal to the radius times 2. So, the diameter for this circle is 4 × 2 = 8. Therefore, the approximate circumference is: 3.14 × 8 = 25.12

373) The correct answer is D. Area of a circle ≈ 3.14 × radius^2. The radius of this circle is 6, and 6^2 = 36. Therefore, the area is approximately: 36 × 3.14 = 113.04

374) The correct answer is B. The area of circle A is 0.4^2 × 3.14 = 0.16 × 3.14 = 0.5024. The area of circle B is 0.2^2 × 3.14 = 0.04 × 3.14 = 0.1256. Then subtract: 0.5024 − 0.1256 = 0.3768

375) The correct answer is D. The volume of a box is calculated by taking the length times the width times the height: 5 × 6 × 10 = 300

376) The correct answer is B. Triangle area = (base × height) ÷ 2. Substitute the amounts for base and height: area = (5 × 2) ÷ 2 = 10 ÷ 2 = 5

377) The correct answer is B. Cone volume = (3.14 × radius^2 × height) ÷ 3. Substitute the values for base and height. volume = (3.14 × 3^2 × 4) ÷ 3 = (3.14 × 9 × 4) ÷ 3 = 3.14 × 36 ÷ 3 = 37.68

378) The correct answer is B. Remember that the perimeter is the measurement along the outside edges of the rectangle or other area. The formula for perimeter is as follows: P = 2W + 2L. If the room is 12 feet by 10 feet, we need 12 feet × 2 to finish the long sides of the room and 10 feet × 2 to finish the shorter sides of the room. (2 × 10) + (2 × 12) = 20 + 24 = 44. Each piece of wood is one foot long, so 44 pieces are needed to finish the room.

379) The correct answer is A. First, we have to calculate the total square footage available.
If there are 4 rooms which are 10 by 10 each: 4 × (10 × 10) = 400 square feet in total

Now calculate the square footage of the new rooms:
20 × 10 = 200
2 rooms × (10 × 8) = 160
200 + 160 = 360 total square feet for the new rooms

So, the remaining square footage for the bathroom is calculated by taking the total minus the square footage of the new rooms: 400 − 360 = 40 square feet left. Since each existing room is 10 feet long, we know that the new bathroom also needs to be 10 feet long in order to fit in. So, the new bathroom measures 4 feet × 10 feet.

380) The correct answer is A. The area of a circle is 3.14 × radius^2. Radius is half of diameter, and in our problem the diameter is 36, so the radius is 18. So, put the values into the formula to solve: 3.14 × 18 × 18 = 1,017

381) The correct answer is A. Step 1 – Calculate the average high temperature in Celsius: (12 + 13 + 17) ÷ 3 = 42 ÷ 3 = 14°C average. Step 2 – Convert the average in Celsius to Fahrenheit using the formula provided. °F = 1.8(°C) + 32 = 1.8(14°) + 32 = 25.2 + 32 = 57.2° F.

382) The correct answer is D. Step 1 – Calculate the rate in terms of a daily percentage: 72.8% ÷ 182 days = 0.4% per day. Step 2 – Divide this amount into 100% to find the approximate number of days in total: 100% ÷ 0.4% per day = 250 days in total. Step 3 – Subtract to determine how many days remain: 250 − 182 = 68 days left

383) The correct answer is D. At 11:00, 30 minutes (or half an hour) will have passed. If he is traveling 70 miles per hour, he will have travel 35 miles in this half hour (70 × ½ = 35). If he was 140 miles from Farnam when he saw the sign, we need to subtract 35 miles from this to get the answer: 140 − 35 = 105 miles from Farnam

384) The correct answer is C. At 12:30, two hours will have passed and he will have traveled 140 miles (70 miles per hour × 2 hours = 140 total miles). Georgetown was 210 miles away when he saw the sign, so subtract to find out how far he is from Georgetown: 210 − 140 = 70 miles from Georgetown

385) The correct answer is C. From the previous question, we know that at 12:30 he is 70 miles from Georgetown without having taken a break. If he is traveling 70 miles per hour, he would need only 1 more hour to get to Georgetown at 1:30 if he had not taken a break. But we need to add in a 30 minute break, so he would arrive in Georgetown at 2:00 pm.

386) The correct answer is D. Add the amounts for the first three bars together: 1.5 + 1.2 + 0.8 = 3.5

387) The correct answer is B. The median is the middle value when the values in the data set are in ascending order. So, put the values in ascending order first of all: 0.8, 1, 1, 1, 1, 1.2, 1.2, 1.3, 1.5. The median is the one in the middle: 0.8, 1, 1, 1, **1**, 1.2, 1.2, 1.3, 1.5

388) The correct answer is A. The range is the highest value minus the lowest value: 1.5 − 0.8 = 0.7

389) The correct answer is C. For one recipe, we need ¼ cup of flour and ½ cup of sugar, which is equal to ¾ when combined. We are doubling the recipe, so we need ¾ × 2 = 1½ cups.

390) The correct answer is A. The recipe is for 4 brownies, but we only want to make 2 brownies, so we have to use half of the ingredients. ½ cup of sugar is needed for the original recipe, but we only want half of this: ½ × ½ = ¼

391) The correct answer is B. The original recipe was for 4 brownies but we are making 6 brownies, so we can set up the following fraction to get our proportion: 6/4 = 4/4 + 2/4 = 1 + ½ = 1½. For 6 brownies, we need to use 1½ of all of the ingredients listed on the original recipe: ½ teaspoon × 1½ = [(½ × 1) + (½ × ½)] = ½ + ¼ = ¾

392) The correct answer is D. 3 tablespoons of cocoa powder and ¼ teaspoon of baking powder are needed for the original recipe to make 4 brownies. There are 3 teaspoons in a tablespoon, so calculate the total teaspoons needed for the original recipe first: 3 tablespoons × 3 = 9 teaspoons cocoa powder + ¼ teaspoon baking powder = 9¼ teaspoons in total. We are now making 12 brownies, so we need to multiply all of the ingredients by 3: 9¼ × 3 = 27¾ teaspoons

393) The correct answer is A. The scores were: 9.9, 9.9, 8.2, 7.6 and 6.8. Put them in ascending order and highlight the one in the middle: 6.8, 7.6, **8.2**, 9.9, 9.9

394) The correct answer is B. The range is the highest amount minus the lowest amount: 91 – 54 = 37

395) The correct answer is D. Our points are (5, 7) and (11, –3) so use the midpoint formula.
$(x_1 + x_2) \div 2$, $(y_1 + y_2) \div 2$
(5 + 11) ÷ 2 = midpoint x, (7 – 3) ÷ 2 = midpoint y
16 ÷ 2 = midpoint x, 4 ÷ 2 = midpoint y
8 = midpoint x, 2 = midpoint y

396) The correct answer is A. First, find the relationship between each of the numbers.
7 + 7 = 14
14 + 7 = 21
21 + 7 = 28
Therefore, we have to add 7 to 28 in order to find the solution.
28 + 7 = 35

397) The correct answer is C. Substitute –2 for x to solve.
$2x^2 - x + 5 =$
[2 × (–2²)] – (–2) + 5 =
[2 × (4)] – (–2) + 5 =
(2 × 4) + 2 + 5 =
8 + 2 + 5 = 15

398) The correct answer is A. Isolate x to solve. You do this by doing the same operation on each side of the equation. First, subtract 5 from each side to get rid of the integer 5 on the left side.
–6x + 5 = –19
–6x + 5 – 5 = –19 – 5

Then simplify.
–6x + 5 – 5 = –19 – 5
–6x = –24
Then divide each side by –6 to isolate x.
–6x = –24
–6x ÷ –6 = –24 ÷ –6
x = –24 ÷ –6
x = 4

399) The correct answer is A. Perform the multiplication on the terms in the parentheses.
2(3x – 1) = 4(x + 1) – 3
6x – 2 = (4x + 4) – 3
Then simplify.
6x – 2 = (4x + 4) – 3
6x – 2 = 4x + 1
6x – 2 – 1 = 4x + 1 – 1
6x – 3 = 4x
Then isolate x to get your answer.
6x – 3 = 4x
6x – 4x – 3 = 4x – 4x
2x – 3 = 0
2x – 3 + 3 = 0 + 3
2x = 3
2x ÷ 2 = 3 ÷ 2
$x = {}^3/_2$

400) The correct answer is C. Each term contains the variables x and y. So, factor out xy as shown: $2xy - 8x^2y + 6y^2x^2 = xy(2 - 8x + 6xy)$. Then, factor out any whole numbers. All of the terms inside the parentheses are divisible by 2, so factor out 2: $xy(2 - 8x + 6xy) = 2xy(1 - 4x + 3xy)$

ANSWER KEY

1) C
2) D
3) D
4) C
5) B
6) A
7) B
8) C
9) D
10) D
11) A
12) C
13) B
14) C
15) A
16) D
17) A
18) C
19) B
20) B
21) D
22) D
23) D
24) C
25) C
26) A
27) A
28) B
29) C
30) D
31) B
32) A
33) D
34) D
35) C
36) D
37) C
38) C
39) D
40) C
41) B
42) D
43) A
44) B
45) B
46) D
47) A
48) B
49) D
50) A
51) A
52) A
53) A
54) B
55) C
56) C

57) D	86) D
58) A	87) B
59) C	88) A
60) D	89) C
61) B	90) A
62) B	91) D
63) A	92) A
64) D	93) D
65) A	94) C
66) A	95) B
67) B	96) A
68) C	97) A
69) D	98) D
70) C	99) B
71) A	100) C
72) B	101) C
73) D	102) B
74) A	103) B
75) C	104) C
76) D	105) B
77) B	106) B
78) B	107) B
79) D	108) C
80) D	109) D
81) D	110) D
82) A	111) A
83) B	112) B
84) A	113) B
85) C	114) A

115) C
116) B
117) B
118) D
119) B
120) B
121) C
122) C
123) C
124) D
125) A
126) B
127) A
128) B
129) C
130) A
131) A
132) D
133) D
134) C
135) C
136) C
137) D
138) C
139) B
140) B
141) D
142) A
143) A

144) D
145) B
146) B
147) D
148) C
149) B
150) D
151) C
152) D
153) C
154) A
155) C
156) C
157) D
158) C
159) B
160) B
161) C
162) A
163) B
164) D
165) C
166) C
167) C
168) B
169) B
170) C
171) C
172) A

173) B
174) B
175) D
176) C
177) B
178) C
179) C
180) A
181) A
182) A
183) B
184) B
185) C
186) B
187) C
188) D
189) C
190) C
191) A
192) B
193) D
194) C
195) A
196) D
197) B
198) A
199) C
200) C
201) B

202) D
203) C
204) C
205) D
206) C
207) C
208) A
209) C
210) B
211) B
212) D
213) B
214) C
215) B
216) C
217) D
218) D
219) C
220) A
221) B
222) C
223) B
224) C
225) C
226) A
227) A
228) C
229) A
230) B

231) B
232) C
233) A
234) A
235) D
236) A
237) C
238) D
239) C
240) D
241) C
242) B
243) B
244) D
245) C
246) B
247) A
248) A
249) C
250) A
251) D
252) C
253) C
254) D
255) A
256) C
257) D
258) B
259) B

260) D
261) A
262) B
263) C
264) D
265) D
266) D
267) C
268) C
269) C
270) D
271) A
272) B
273) B
274) D
275) B
276) D
277) D
278) B
279) B
280) A
281) C
282) A
283) D
284) C
285) C
286) D
287) A
288) B

289) D
290) C
291) B
292) B
293) A
294) D
295) B
296) C
297) B
298) D
299) A
300) D
301) C
302) C
303) B
304) D
305) B
306) D
307) A
308) B
309) B
310) D
311) A
312) C
313) B
314) C
315) D
316) A
317) C

318) D
319) A
320) D
321) A
322) C
323) D
324) D
325) B
326) C
327) C
328) D
329) A
330) D
331) C
332) A
333) C
334) D
335) A
336) C
337) A
338) C
339) B
340) D
341) D
342) C
343) B
344) D
345) A
346) D

347) C
348) A
349) C
350) D
351) D
352) C
353) C
354) B
355) D
356) A
357) B
358) B
359) C
360) A
361) C
362) D
363) A
364) B
365) C
366) C
367) D
368) B
369) A
370) B
371) D
372) C
373) D
374) B
375) D

376) B
377) B
378) B
379) A
380) A
381) A
382) D
383) D
384) C
385) C
386) D
387) B
388) A
389) C
390) A
391) B
392) D
393) A
394) B
395) D
396) A
397) C
398) A
399) A
400) C

APPLIED MATHEMATICS FORMULA SHEET

Weight

1 ounce ≈ 28.350 grams
1 pound = 16 ounces
1 pound ≈ 453.592 grams
1 milligram = 0.001 grams
1 kilogram = 1,000 grams
1 kilogram ≈ 2.2 pounds

Volume

1 cup = 8 fluid ounces
1 quart = 4 cups
1 gallon = 4 quarts
1 gallon = 231 cubic inches
1 liter ≈ 0.264 gallons
1 cubic foot = 1,728 cubic inches
1 cubic yard = 27 cubic feet

Distance

1 foot = 12 inches
1 yard = 3 feet
1 mile = 5,280 feet
1 mile ≈ 1.61 kilometers
1 inch = 2.54 centimeters
1 foot = 0.3048 meters
1 meter = 1,000 millimeters
1 meter = 100 centimeters
1 kilometer = 1,000 meters
1 kilometer ≈ 0.62 miles

Area

1 square foot = 144 square inches
1 square yard = 9 square feet

Circle

number of degrees in circle = 360°
circumference ≈ 3.14 × *diameter*
area ≈ 3.14 × (*radius*)^2

Triangle

sum of angles = 180°
area = ½ (*base* × *height*)

Rectangle

perimeter = 2(*length* + *width*)
area = *length* × *width*

Rectangular Solid (Box)

volume = *length* × *width* × *height*

Cube

volume = (*length of side*)^3

Cylinder

volume ≈ 3.14 × (*radius*)^2 × *height*

Cone

volume ≈ (3.14 × *radius*^{2} × *height*) ÷ 3

Sphere (Ball)

volume ≈ 4/3 × 3.14 × *radius*^{3}

Temperature

°C = 0.56(°F − 32) or 5/9(°F − 32)
°F = 1.8(°C) + 32 or (9/5 × °C) + 32

www.ingramcontent.com/pod-product-compliance
Lightning Source LLC
Chambersburg PA
CBHW081351080526
44588CB00016B/2450